10/93

M W
& R

SCHOOL'S OUT

The Catastrophe in
Public Education and
What We Can Do About It

ANDREW NIKIFORUK

MACFARLANE WALTER & ROSS
TORONTO

Macfarlane Walter & Ross
37A Hazelton Avenue
Toronto, Canada M5R 2E3

Canadian Cataloguing in Publication Data

Nikiforuk, Andrew, 1955–
   School's out: the catastrophe in public education
and what we can do about it

Includes bibliographical references and index.
ISBN 0–921912–48–X

I. Education - Canada. I. Title.

LA412.N55 1993   370'.971   C93–094899–8

Printed in the United States of America

To my boys, Aidan and Keegan,
and their children's children, the generations I write for

Education in the true sense, of course, is an enablement to serve both the living human community in its natural household or neighborhood and the precious cultural possessions that the living community inherits or should inherit. To educate is, literally, to "bring up," to bring young people to a responsible maturity, to help them to be good caretakers of what they have been given, to help them to be charitable toward fellow creatures. Such an education is obviously pleasant and useful to have; that a sizable number of humans should have it is probably also one of the necessities of human life in this world. And if this education is to be used well, it is obvious that it must be used some where; *it must be used where one lives, where one intends to continue to live; it must be brought home.*

WENDELL BERRY

Contents

Acknowledgements

This book has three important intellectual mentors: Wendell Barry, Jacques Ellul, and Jacques Barzun. These men care as passionately about teaching and learning as they do about the sanctity of the word.

The *Globe and Mail* deserves a hearty thanks, here, too for standing by my educational column on the Facts and Arguments page.

The soul of this book reflects the overwhelming and phenomenal readership response to the *Globe* column. In particular I wish to thank Dr. Joe Freedman, Carl Kline, Sheila Morrison, Maureen Somers-Beebe, Marjorie Gann, Helen Raham, Malkin Dare, Josef Macek, John Reeder, and hundreds of other parents and teachers who have written or phoned in the last year. I hope this book reflects their common sense as eloquently and urgently as they expressed it.

As for my publishers and editors, they have been more than patient and thorough. Few individuals in the publishing world practise their trade as professionally as Jan Walter and Gary Ross. Their commitment to excellence in books has certainly blessed this one. Wendy Thomas's keen and critical eye as copy editor simply made it a leaner and clearer read.

Every book has a quiet shepherdess and, as in all my writing projects, this role has been filled by Doreen Docherty, my wife, partner, lover, confidante, and critic. While I wrote at all hours of the day and night, she indefatigably kept our household running and our boys employed by adventures both funny and moving. Her many sacrifices made this book possible. With her Hebridean determination and energy, I have learned that the difficulties and opportunities that life announces each day can best be met with laughter and love.

Introduction

North America's educational system has fallen from grace,
not with an angelic flutter but with a thud. If the U.S.
school system resembles a homeless beggar on the streets
of New York, Canada's expensive counterpart defensively limps
along in a state of humiliation and confusion. Our schools are far
from what people expect them to be. This book begins with no
illusions and no lies.

I am not an expert on education. I am, however, a father, a former teacher, and a writer. From such ground I have written this
book with equal measures of anger, regret, and hopefulness. My
anger, which admittedly drives this polemic, comes from my awareness as a father of two boys that some parents have totally abandoned the public school system while others have been shut out of
it by administrators. My regret stems from an awareness, gained as
a special education teacher, that my fellow tradesmen did not
always speak up against the administrative and bureaucratic out-
rages that altered their workplaces years ago.

My hopefulness springs not from any belief that educators alone
can repair the damage, but from a commitment to providing anti-
dotes to despair. Schools may look like alien monoliths, but they
can be changed by common people for the common good.

This small book bears witness to a catastrophe in public education that many teachers and parents now regard as this century's most poorly reported news story. There are, of course, many fine and dedicated teachers. And there are still many good schools and many good school boards in North America, but they have become harder to find than governments without debt. Educators, of course, deny this reality, just as they robotically deny the cruel ability of modern fads, bureaucratic meddling, and floating standards to cheat our children of an education.

The continent's educational élites now mimic the deafness and blindness of North America's traditional power brokers. They seem incapable of admitting failure (it's not part of the progressive vocabulary) but proficient at thwarting reform that might end their reign of miseducation. In a small way, I hope this book can help retire a few "itinerant professional vandals," school administrators who live far from the classroom disasters they create for our children.

I have consciously addressed this book not to the decision makers but to those who now live with the consequences of their bad decisions: parents and teachers. Schools cannot change for the better until these two often warring groups align themselves against the political powers and economic forces that have neutered the school as a place of community-minded instruction and made each camp a glib scapegoat for school failure. As such, *School's Out* is a populist manifesto for those who work in schools and those who depend on their results. This explains why I have designed this book as part argument, part history, and part practical guide to change.

Unlike many educational critics, I do not believe that the public education system should be destroyed, replaced by vouchers, or even retooled to meet the vague and vain requirements of "global competitiveness." I have written this book in hopes of helping to restore purpose and clarity to what was once a noble idea: schooling on common ground for the common good. The public education system must be saved, not discarded.

Both American and Canadian schools appear in this book. As the Toronto educator Des Dixon has pointed out, the two school systems are "twins with the same genetic defects." The only real difference is that the Canadian sibling suffers from a ten-year development lag. As an insecure brother without a real national curriculum, Canada seems intent on replaying the California-inspired mayhem south of the border.

Although I have included in *School's Out* portions of some of my *Globe and Mail* columns on education, this book is an original work. I wrote it not to incorporate old material but to give my columns ground underfoot. From the beginning I intended the book to be short and abrupt. Too much bunkum has already been written about education in the last decade; I have no desire to add to what has become a very smelly pile of academic rubbish.

Readers looking for ideological purity in this volume will likely be very frustrated. The great intellectual schisms of the day no longer fall into right-wing or left-wing camps. Although good schools have always managed to transcend these battles, they cannot escape the new ideological struggles defining our culture (or lack of it). In one corner, wearing an entirely new set of wings, stand the dispossessed: those who value community, particular virtues, and the populist traditions of resistance against tyranny. On the other side, equipped with mechanical wings, are the modernists: those who replace real communities with global villages, universalism, and technology. This book sides unequivocally with community and tradition. "Continuity is at the heart of conservatism," says the American biologist Garett Hardin, and ecology, the caring for home places and home economies, "serves that heart."

My layman credentials for writing this polemic partly stem from my experiences as a special education teacher in Toronto and Winnipeg. For several years I taught a variety of students, from all classes, how to read, write, compute, and think. Nearly a decade ago I left the classroom, because I no longer wanted to be part of a system that cared more about public relations than relating to community life and the plain virtues of teaching and learning.

As a roving student I also acquired another kind of fundamental school lore. Thanks to the mobile character of my father's career (he taught dentistry), I attended more than twenty public, Catholic, and private schools in North America and Europe. This jarring school life, which included a stint in California, gave me a sharp eye and ear for good schools as well as a respect for rootedness.

Finally, I have no doubt that this book will be misread, as my columns have been, as either a total refutation of progressive education or as some quaint plea to return to the 1950s — a fretful and disturbing decade that I am not very familiar with. Neither interpretation is just. I believe that respecting children's interests and using a variety of pedagogical tools to engage them in learning are good advances in schooling. But I support these ideas only in the context of pursuing high standards while learning real subjects with committed teachers. Some progressive classrooms meet these goals. But, too often, I have witnessed the progressive or modern school as a lacklustre place where getting by for the moment is the minimum virtue demanded of pupils and teachers.

Such poverty of purpose makes a public school system vulnerable to attack, if not dismemberment. No community and no nation can finance aimlessness in the classroom without losing soul and heart. Yet many schools now present this very danger to our communities.

ANDREW NIKIFORUK
Calgary, May 1993

CHAPTER I

What Are Schools For?

*"To remain ignorant of things that happened before
you were born is to remain a child."* CICERO

WISE COUNTENANCE AND STOUT HEART

The first school had a hearth and was called home. The kitchen, the field, or the workshop served as an informal classroom. A peasant shoemaker taught his son how to be a peasant shoemaker; the peasant's spouse taught her daughter how to be a peasant's wife. So it remains to this day. Each family has a curriculum; each home is a child's first school.

In ancient Greece a school — the word comes from the Greek *skholē*, meaning "freedom from business activities" — was any place where citizens met in leisure to learn and debate. Above all, it was a place where discourse flourished and intelligent speech demanded intelligent listening. Ultimately, it was a place where the spoken and written word was respected.

The much-heralded Athenian school system existed only for the male children of the privileged; slaves, women, and artisans did not attend. Philosophers such as Aristotle, Plato, and Socrates spoke much about education, but their ideas had little influence on the working of these schools. Like most ancient pedagogical institutions, Athenian classrooms focused on cultivating excellence (*arete*) and developing strong moral character. Music and physical training shared equal time with reading, writing, and rhetoric. The heroic poems of Homer and the populist fables of Aesop served not only as literary training but as moral instruction in whole-mindedness or temperance.

The real point of Greek education, as the French historian Henri Marrou noted, "was to teach the child to transcend himself... Accordingly '*paideia*' was not a pedagogical method for rearing children but a preparation for the ultimate goal, '*humanitas*' (becoming a man.)" What distinguished the schools of Athens, then and now, was that they tried to make excellent citizens. As for people who took no interest in education or in the improvement of public behaviour, the Athenians had a word for them: *idiōtēs*, or idiots.

On this continent, the first compulsory public school system sprouted not in Boston or Toronto but amid fields of thorny cactus in the city of Mexico. Long before Horace Mann and Egerton Ryerson ever dreamed of common schooling for the white settlers of North America, the Aztecs had achieved this republican goal with an aristocratic clarity of purpose.

The Aztecs (or Nahuas, as they called themselves), who combined a mystical, war-like view of the world with a genuine humanism, had two words for education: *Tlacahuapahualiztli* (the art of strengthening or bringing up men) and *Neixtlamachiliztli* (the art of giving wisdom to the face). The goal of both arts was not to glorify the individual but to integrate young people into the highest ideals of community and state. Training girls or boys in the spiritual and cultural heritage of the past not only guaranteed concurrence to law (the giving up of oneself to what is appropriate and righteous) but also upheld discipline, austerity, and hard work, the cultural blood of Nahuatl life.

After rigorous and prolonged training in the home on the importance of strength and self-control, all Aztec children, rich and poor, entered one of two grammar-like schools. The *Calmécac* focused on intellectual growth and priestly wisdoms; the *Telpochcalli* trained men for the practical rigours of war and women for the arts of weaving and embroidery. School commonly took place in a religious temple, which emphasized the moral and sacred intent of teaching and learning.

At the *Calmécac*, students cleaned their own classrooms, cooked their own meals, and prayed daily. They studied the art of good speaking, the wisdom of flower and song (poetry), the principles of good government, and the divinity of astrological study. After a scanty breakfast, the teachers or wise men would begin the lessons of the day with a magnanimity of purpose. They sought to teach the children how they should live; how to respect others; how to dedicate themselves to what was good and righteous; how to avoid evil; and how "to flee unrighteousness with strength, refraining from perversion and greed."

The Aztecs' noble object of giving youth "wise countenance" and "stout heart" floundered after the Spanish conquest in the late sixteenth century, when the conquistadores destroyed Nahuatl schools and executed or banished their priestly teachers. With the ruination of the Aztec educational system, many Christian missionaries observed a profound change in the behaviour of Mexican youth: they now drank too much fermented maguey juice and appeared heartless. In a final appearance before the victorious Cortés, the teachers declared, "If, as you say, our gods are dead, it is better that you allow us to die too."

Nahuatl culture upheld much that was horrific to European eyes, including the ritualistic sacrifice of fifty thousand people a year, but it appreciated the value of schools. When these institutions died, so did the flower and song of Nahuatl culture.

Today, four hundred years after the Aztecs championed the idea of obligatory schooling, it's unlikely that any invading power might consider the destruction of North America's public school system as an efficient way to silence our hearts and traditions. In fact, a modern-day Cortés might well conclude that the best way to subdue the peoples of North America would be to leave their school system intact, for it has become a powerful weapon of cultural dismemberment.

THE LIMITS OF SCHOOLING

All ancient schools — whether Greek, Egyptian, or Mayan — knew their place and their limits. As private institutions, they primarily served the male children of élites, who paid for and selected schools with no more care than do most parents today. All early schools primarily focused on basic skills, particularly reading, writing, and arithmetic.

More importantly, all early schools acted as gatekeepers. They controlled the flow of cultural information, separating the trivial from the meaningful, the traditional from the modern, the sacred from the profane. They strove to protect children from idolatry, the worship of images and the celebration of thoughtlessness. These early schools may not always have selected curricula that achieved these ends but the object of selection was always to encourage the learning of wisdom.

As largely religious or moral institutions, ancient schools tried to teach youth — the inheritors of tradition, memory, and culture — to place a distance between wants and needs. They generally admonished against the accumulation of wealth and the exclusive preoccupation with the present or the self. They did so to keep their communities whole; the ancients knew that any schooling that encouraged citizens to be totally free of religious heritage or historical tradition would spread a cultural cholera among the people. To the ancients, a school that eviscerated life, faith, and community was antithetical to the very idea of school. In the end, Athens lost its school system to the sophists, teachers who called themselves wise men but did not come from the communities in which they taught. Foreigners in tradition and spirit, the sophists strove to train Athenians for careers of glory and profit. In so doing, they often offended the local sensibility, charging grandly for a service that ultimately fragmented the community.

Sophists, the original peddlers of relevance and relativity, did not believe in anything or anybody. Man, wrote Protagoras, a leading sophist, "is the measure of all things, both of the seen and the unseen." The modern school, with its eyes turned to the future and its focus on "relevant activities," walks the crooked road of sophistry. The sophists loved pretentious argument, word play, and process. They turned athletic training away from the celebration of health to the glorification of self. And they turned schooling from a means of strengthening the traditions and spirit of community into the pursuit of individual happiness, much as we've done in our schools.

PAINFUL LESSONS

Modern educators like to dwell on the brutality and unpleasantness of the early schools. In ancient Egypt, students strove to become scribes, engineers, or architects by labouring tediously over one thousand characters on papyrus. The Egyptians advised their young to "give thy heart to learning and love her like a mother," but the children's instructors shared no such illusions. Teachers believed that "a boy's ears are on his back; he hears when he is beaten."

In ancient China the schools rewarded stoics. Chinese classrooms, typically located in a house or temple, consisted of little more than an armchair for an ill-paid teacher and an altar to Confucius; students bowed to both. They also brought their own books, paper, and India ink, using them for copying sacred texts to memorize. Many pupils attended school from sunrise to five o'clock in the afternoon with the hope of passing several infamous examinations that led eventually to offices of profit or honour, and finally to the Imperial Academy or "Forest of Pencils."

The Athenian classroom bore all the dreary characteristics of the Chinese. Slaves, called *paidagogos*, accompanied male children to school, carried their satchels, upheld good manners, and protected them from the sexual advances of other men. Even though the pedagogues held a more important role in the moral education of youth than did the schoolmasters, Athenians held pedagogues in contempt. More often than not, these child-care workers got the job because of their mental or physical unfitness to do anything else. Upon seeing a slave fall from a tree and break his leg, Pericles observed, "Lo, he is now a pedagogue." The true *paidagogos* of our day are the legions of poorly paid, badly trained day-care workers.

Any rogue or scoundrel in need of money could establish a school in Athens, and many did. Subservient to the whims of their clients and chained to what Athenians called a "trail of cheapness," the schoolmasters were held in even lower esteem than the pedagogues. Seated in a highback chair in front of rows of hard benches, these indigent misfits straightened out the disobedient "with threats and beatings like a warped and twisted plank," as Plato wrote.

In Roman schools, bloody floggings were so common that the phrase *"manum subducere ferulae"* (to withdraw the hand from the swish of the rod) became a euphemism for dropping out of school. Even in Nahuatl classrooms, discipline frequently demanded blood; refractory students had their legs, ears, chest, or thighs pierced with cactus thorns.

The presence of clubs, whips, or bamboo poles in early schools did not reflect on the skills and subjects being taught. It did, however, illustrate that punishment and chastisement pervaded all spheres of life in many ancient civilizations, and that the school, then as now, faithfully mirrored the societal reality. The prevalence of beatings also suggests that, then as now, talk without chalk could be dreary and instruction without coherence mind-numbing. Most teachers know that classroom discipline is mainly a function of good teaching; where this is absent, the rod has been substituted. All through history, good teachers have been in short supply.

Modern educators sometimes cite such grisly practices to disparage the whole history of schooling, rather than accepting that any historic institution is a sedimentary mixture of the noble and the ignoble. Although many ancient schools did indeed operate like prisons, educational progress has always had an elusive character. In many cases, modern schools have merely replaced physical forms of abuse with emotional and pedagogical ones. Despite the development of good scientific knowledge about what kind of teaching works best with children, modern educators routinely follow their own whims and still use methods that cause unnecessary failure in reading and math. They abruptly change classroom practices in the name of relevance without ever seeking the consent of parents for these social and pedagogical experiments. And, in place of the cane, they now employ subtle therapeutic exercises such as "values clarification" to shape children's moral lives. The climate of many North American schools has become so foul, meanwhile, that violence directed against teachers and other students has once again made these schools unsafe.[1] The threat of overt physical discipline may have disappeared, but it has been replaced by indignities and injustices as brutalizing as any whip.

THE EARLY IDEAL

What North Americans hold true or dear about school springs not from Athens or Mexico City, but from the writings of the Roman orator and master teacher, Quintilian. Unlike most Roman teachers of rhetoric in the years after Christ's crucifixion, Quintilian was respected for his common sense and concern for character development. His writings about quality education helped build the populist notion of what good schooling is all about. Horace Mann admired Quintilian so greatly that he infused the common school with much of the Roman's wisdom.

Unlike many of his contemporaries, Quintilian believed that all children could learn, "for no one is found who has not profited at all by study." He affirmed the importance of elementary education, of training in the basics (reading, writing, and arithmetic) beginning at age seven. Foreshadowing the idea of kindergarten, he believed that early teaching should involve some form of play to avoid that "one who cannot yet love studies should come to hate all learning."

Quintilian preferred public instruction at school to private tutoring at home for a variety of reasons. Good teachers delight in crowded classrooms, he believed, and at school a pupil can "hear many things approved, many things corrected; he will profit by another's sloth rebuked, another's industry commended." He also valued public instruction as a means to promote healthy rivalry among striving pupils and to keep track of progress with regular tests. He valued physical exercise as a means of refreshing and restoring pupils' mental energy. In contrast to most of his peers, he loathed corporal punishment, believing that violence begets violence.

His definition of a good teacher remains unequalled in the inflated library of educational rhetoric: "He must have no vices himself and tolerate none in his pupils. Let him be stern but not melancholy, friendly but not familiar, lest in the one case he incur dislike, in the other contempt. He must constantly dwell upon the honourable and the good; for the more he admonishes his pupils the less he will require to punish them. He must never lose his temper, yet he will not pass over what deserves correction; he must be simple in his teaching, able to endure hard toil, persevering rather than exacting."

As for the duties of pupils, Quintilian was equally explicit and clear-minded: "They should love their teachers no less than their studies themselves and should regard them as the parents not indeed of their bodies but of their minds." There can be no fruitful learning, he concluded, "save by the harmonious co-operation of him who gives and him who receives instruction."

Because most teachers today are effectively asked to construct their own theories about schooling, the unnamed spirit of Quintilian exists only in the public imagination. And because few beginning teachers ever receive a course in the history or philosophy of education, most don't know, as Quintilian did, that there are no new pedagogical problems under the sun.

THE GREAT DIDACTIC

In the five centuries between the fall of Rome and the beginning of the Renaissance, school as a voluntary and private institution fell into a sort of darkness. But with the invention of the printing press in the early sixteenth century, school again came to life as a means to organize and limit the amount of information on the loose. Before the printing press, England had but thirty-four schools; soon after Gutenberg, 444 schools had sprouted across the country. As one of America's foremost educational critics, Neil Postman, argues, the modern school took form in the seventeenth century as a "means of governing the ecology of information." The multiplication of books on varying subjects merely accelerated the demand for more schools. Although never advertised as such, the idea of universal public education was in fact a spirited public defence against a free-market flood of information.

One of the advocates of this school explosion was John Amos Comenius, a Moravian Brethren and seventeenth-century father of the textbook. As a great teacher and writer, the Czech-speaking Comenius believed that education was about knowledge, virtue, and piety. In hundreds of essays and texts, he tried to give "an accurate anatomy of the universe, dissecting the veins and limbs of all things in such a way that there shall be nothing that is not seen, and that each part shall appear in its proper place and without confusion." Unlike the designers of modern textbooks, which often present the reader with unrelated trivia, Comenius understood that the purpose of instruction was clarity, straightforwardness, and discrimination. He championed "the School of the Mother's Knee" and his master work, *The Great Didactic*, published in Latin in 1657, contains more practical wisdom about teaching than most faculties of education. As the producer of the first illustrated school books for children, Comenius recognized that the textbook was the most efficient and stable means of conserving traditional ideas against eroding waves of trivia and data.

In abandoning Comenius's gift to education by either banning textbooks altogether or using dumb collections of saleable entertainment, the modern school has ceased to be a gatekeeper. Awash in information, data, and fads, it has become a place where the seeds of learning, virtue, and religion drown and the ideals of Comenius founder. Modern educators, having turned their backs on the difficult pursuit of wisdom, signal their folly by declaring allegiance to technocratic ideals: the "process of learning" and "learning to learn." With no gates and no priorities, the modern school stands nowhere and for nothing.

The proliferation of early schools was fed not only by society's need to control the flow of information (in order to retain some commonness) but also by the rapid dismemberment of the family. As the Industrial Revolution took fathers away from the field and the neighbourhood shop, their capacity to teach their own children was sharply limited. In 1810, 87 per cent of all fathers worked at or near the home, where they could be tutors and trainers. By the turn of the last century, the fraction had declined to 42 per cent; as we approach the turn of another century, the fraction stands at 3 per cent. Obeying the dictates of capitalist or socialist materialism, many fathers now spend, by one estimate, an average of seventeen seconds per day in intimate conversation with their children.

The movement for public schooling was, in short, a social invention to repair the destruction of an old tradition: familial instruction or job training. Today, with more and more mothers leaving the household for the workplace, school can't help but become less a place for teaching and learning and more a place for child rearing and infant therapy. This abandonment of the nurturing of children to strangers with certificates and degrees, an unprecedented social experiment, is frequently celebrated as progress. In truth, it is the work of a self-interested and materialistic generation that knows little history and possesses little wisdom.

THE LITTLE RED SCHOOLHOUSE

North Americans had a romance with school when it was red and little and unconsciously devoted to the Greek ideal of *skholē*. Many of the original one-room schoolhouses were unused barns, abandoned meeting places, empty chicken coops, small churches, or wagon sheds. Most children walked a mile to get to school. They rarely attended more than six months a year or six years in total. The basic curriculum consisted of "reading and 'riting and religion." In the little red schoolhouse, "discipline" often meant what it no longer means: learning how to be a disciple and to receive instruction from another.

Not surprisingly, most early North American schools existed to teach children about the Bible, so they could read it and quote from it. As the only book that most North American families owned, it was the original North American school text. Biblical narratives nourished a common moral discourse and helped create a common culture. From the Bible and the strength of sacred words all other books flowed, and all other Western ideas took shape. Abraham Lincoln educated himself by reading the Bible, Shakespeare, and Euclid. The highest hope that every parent had for a child was that he or she would become as wise as Solomon. The idea of sending a child to school to become competent in a specialty, or to feel good about himself, or to prepare for material success, would have struck the early pioneers as demonic.

In the one-room schoolhouse all ages and all classes mixed. Apprenticeships mattered, and young students watched older ones master difficult things and elder students helped the young. The boys sharpened quill pens with their pocketknives, thereby starting a tradition of carrying "penknives" to school. Teachers admonished, "What you are to be, you are now becoming," and "Time is short." Students helped to cut firewood for the stove and parents often took turns feeding or housing the teacher, who generally earned a living by moonlighting. "Only spirit can teach," wrote Ralph Waldo Emerson, and the little red schoolhouse often hummed with spirit.

THE FOUNDING SPIRIT

Horace Mann, one of the founders of the common public school in the nineteenth century, championed the little red schoolhouse and tried to make it universal. As director of the Massachusetts Board of Education, he promoted the idea of state-funded schooling, advocating many good principles along with a few bad ones. Like contemporary educators, he over-inflated the importance of universal schooling, an error that has since been magnified tenfold. He argued, for instance, that a public school system could end poverty, banish crime, promote good health, sow virtue, and generally evaporate discord between the haves and the have-nots. Like many common school advocates, he saw city-making and the machine economy as evil forces tearing apart local life and community. And he partly designed the common school as a first line of defence against these progressive forces.

Though Mann may have overestimated the social good common schooling could achieve and even its defensive capabilities against technological progress, he had a much better idea about what made schools work than most modern administrators. He strongly believed that the common school should provide a general and not a practical education. "The man is the trunk, occupations and professions are only different qualities of the fruit it should yield." He considered the rudiments of knowledge to be arithmetic, English grammar, geography, reading, writing and spelling, human physiology, and vocal music. Propriety of demeanour and principles of duty he also gave high priority in the curriculum.

Mann believed that the common school should stand as an extension of parental authority and, consequently, could not teach virtues not held by the community. To avoid political wrangling and pollution by special interests, he advised schools to follow a simple dictum: "When in doubt, leave it out." Only public governance of the schools through local civil agencies could preserve the "commonness" and community spirit of schools.

Mann plainly understood that schools were self-governing communities that achieved goodness with difficulty and hard work. Experience, he wrote, proved "that there is no necessary connection between literary competency, aptness to teach, and the power to manage and govern a school successfully. They are independent qualifications; yet a marked deficiency in any one of the three, renders the others nearly valueless."

Mann had the highest regard for teachers and considered teaching "the most difficult of arts, and the profoundest of sciences." Not only should teachers be able to teach subjects (as opposed to manuals), they should be able to motivate students and touch the uncommon mind. He believed, as most North Americans still do, that teachers should be virtuous people.

Mann also had a clear sense of the fragile ecology of a school in educating men and women in a democracy. "We may as well attempt to escape from our own personal identity," he wrote, "as to shake off the threefold relation which we bear to others, — the relation of an associate with our contemporaries; of a beneficiary of our ancestors; of a guardian to those who, in the sublime order of Providence, are to follow us." To shirk these manifest duties by not passing on the intellectual and moral property that sustains community was selfishness of the highest order. To Mann this selfishness constituted an "embezzlement and pillage of children."

Mann believed that only the "dormancy and deadness" of local communities could kill the idea of a common school. He understood that any abandonment of the school really meant a disowning of community and rejection of public virtue. Very few educators in North America have read Horace Mann; most do not even know who he was. Our schools reflect both this loss of memory and dis-association with community.

THE GREAT CIRCLE OF BENEFICENCE

Egerton Ryerson, the Methodist father of Canada's public schools, read Mann and admired some of his work, but made sure that Canada did not root its school system so deeply in republican ideals or love of community. In 1846 the Common Schools Act established free common schools for all, with textbooks from the ill-named Irish National Schools system. There was not a single Irish air or poem in these texts — nor, for that matter, even a smattering of what would now be called Canadian content. Designed to foster allegiance to Britain, the texts celebrated King and Mother Country. To this day Canadian schools represent a pragmatic robbing of British, American, and French educational ideals. Most of Canada's school textbooks, for example, are still based on models designed by multinational communication companies for school markets in places such as California and Texas.

In both Canada and the United States, the introduction of public schooling was by no means a celebrated event. Many communities resisted the idea well into the last century, even defying guns and militia, because they regarded the invention as a theft of a traditional freedom: home schooling. These fears were not unfounded. Prior to compulsory public schooling, the literacy rate in Massachusetts, for instance, was 98 per cent, a level its public schools have not been able to achieve again. Ontario reached its literacy peak in 1893, when 90 per cent of its citizens were literate, a level the public schools have not been able to achieve since World War Two.[2]

By the 1920s, resistance to public schooling had largely disappeared. The common school took hold and flowered throughout Canada and the United States. The classroom became a place that was relatively peaceful and enjoyable, and the quality of instruction was often very high. Because of job discrimination — women working outside the home were effectively restricted to nursing and teaching — the schools were staffed by some of the most brilliant women of this century. Children learned the rudiments — by this time commonly agreed to mean reading, writing, and arithmetic — and had a sense of doing something worthwhile. Contrary to the claims of some modern educators, many of these schools promoted rigorous thinking as opposed to memorization. One hundred years ago in the Northwest Territories, for example, students typically wrote high school entrance examinations (not multiple choice tests) requiring them to describe in clear prose the importance of ploughing and rolling northern soils or to outline the differences between presidential and parliamentary governments.

The rituals of becoming a good citizen also made the public school a formal and distinct place. In this regard, the traditional school had several virtues. It was small and therefore accountable. It primarily concerned itself with the teaching and learning of a few ideas and intellectual skills that the culture deemed valuable and memorable — or, in Canada's case, that Britain deemed politically correct. The school also had a moral purpose rooted in a strong sense of community-mindedness. Horace Mann's belief that universal schooling was "the great circle of beneficence" often rang true in these schools.

From the public school evolved the high school, a uniquely North American institution that took root at the turn of the century. The ambitions of educators and the concerns of social reformers eager to end child labour united to create a special place for adolescents. In 1903 the National Educational Association, then the leading teachers' organization in American education, spelled out the mission of this new institution: "Every subject which is taught at all in a secondary school should be taught in the same way and to the same extent to every pupil so long as he pursues it, no matter what the probable destination of the pupil may be or at what point his education is to cease." For a long time, only a third of the graduates of public school attended high school; of these, 5 five per cent went on to university. But a high school diploma truly meant something; it certainly commanded more respect than today's three-year university degree.

Until the 1950s, high school remained a special institution that prepared its graduates for a society that valued hard work and civic duty. When attendance became compulsory for all students in the name of equality, the diploma began losing its value. A document that once honoured achievement testified only to the student's endurance. Today, many high schools are little more than marketplaces for the purveyors of sex, Reeboks, and rock and roll.

A PLACE FOR ALL THINGS

The modern school has lost its original energy and purpose. Indistinct and seemingly democratic schools have become incoherent. Their leaders sometimes argue that spelling is unimportant ("only a courtesy to the reader"), or that reading is essentially a nineteenth-century artefact made redundant by the audio-visual world. Moral instruction has been reduced to a technocratic battery of feel-good choices. Teachers are now taught to believe that learning is ultimately the responsibility of the pupil, who is effectively asked to invent his or her reasons for learning. Because school leaders no longer really value knowledge or history, the general curriculum offers de facto therapy with courses in self-esteem and conflict management.

The autonomous, often alienating nature of modern schooling is exacerbated by the fact that teachers rarely live in the communities in which they teach. School administrators act with fiscal and pedagogical irresponsibility, answerable only to themselves. Teachers never get fired, students never fail, and graduates enter the world unprepared for its rigours and complexities. "Now a new type of school is upon me," wrote an Ontario student recently. With high school degrees often printed on counterfeit paper, graduates enter the world believing that a value means only what you want it to mean; that the expression "Dirty Thirties" probably refers to the unwashed; that astrology is a science; that calculators add and subtract; that learning takes no effort or study; and that playing on the keyboards of obsolete computers with third-rate software has somehow prepared one for the school's new mission: "life-long learning."

The modern notion that the school somehow prepares a student for life is misguided and dangerous. Schools of old respected their limitations. Success at school and success in life have never been one and the same. Good schooling may lead to a good life and honest work, but it certainly cannot guarantee them. Albert Einstein, whose kindly poster-face smiles down on many a schoolroom, stumbled so thoroughly in school that his German governess called him Pater Langweil, or Brother Sluggish. The composer Franz Schubert was a poor student. Winston Churchill absolutely hated school, and Franz Kafka dreaded it. Rosa Luxemburg and Simone de Beauvoir loved the classroom and, not surprisingly, made excellent students. Poverty prevented Charles Dickens, Abraham Lincoln, and Mark Twain from entering any one classroom for any length of time. This roster of school success and failure illustrates plainly that failure in school, or failure to attend school, does not mean failure in the world. When able people fail in the classroom, their failure is merely a failure to meet school-like standards and tests.

"A school's worth and integrity depends upon its willingness to call things by their right names," notes the social critic Wendell Berry. But when schooling becomes "education for life" or an attempt to create "perpetual learners," failure implies more than mere academic shortcoming. Educators, no longer able to distinguish between the true *skholē* and the vagaries of everyday life, conclude falsely that they should ban altogether the notion of failure at school.

This modern obsession to make the school a place for all things also encourages educators to forget the limited uses of a school that the Athenians and the Aztecs defined so clearly. The failure to respect these limits, or even to acknowledge the long tradition of teaching and learning, imperils a noble idea. As we approach the end of the century, it's time to acknowledge that public education in North America is a betrayal of our traditions, our communities, and our children. What began as an attempt to make an aristocratic education available to ordinary people has become a self-serving monopoly that promotes idiocy.

CHAPTER TWO

What's Wrong: The New Idiocy

> *"A system that denies the existence of values denies the possibility of education. Relativism, scientism, scepticism, and anti-intellectualism, the four horsemen of the philosophical apocalypse, have produced that chaos in education that will end in the disintegration of the West."*
> ROBERT HUTCHINS

FOUR QUESTIONS

In 1991 Maureen Somers-Beebe, the thirty-three-year-old daughter of a principal and the mother of three boys, asked the board of education in Peterborough, Ontario, four questions. Her queries related to the performance of one of her sons, Adam, who had got an "above average" report card at the end of Grade 3 at South Monaghan School. Above average, she discovered, really meant that her son (and several of his peers) couldn't read two-syllable words or write a sentence, let alone identify one. He had trouble spelling two- and three-letter words.

Somers-Beebe's son and many of his classmates had been unwitting guinea pigs of a popular educational fad called activity-centred learning. Little direct teaching takes place in this method. Instead, children discover math in sandboxes and warm feelings in books, travelling from one fun centre to another like corporate executives at holiday seminars. To help the children in their travels, the teachers act like flight attendants or tour guides.

Somers-Beebe was concerned about the absence of a curriculum and the fad's disappointing effects on student achievement. Along with the other members of a local group called Parents for Education, she asked the principal and superintendent these four questions:

What are our children learning?
How will they learn it?
When will they learn it?
How will you know, the teacher know, and the parent know that the child has learned it?

In response, Somers-Beebe and company received a long talk on early child development theory and a copy of *The Formative Years*, a jargon-filled government guideline on early childhood education. They also heard the four classic brush-offs: parents worry too much; we're the professionals; schools are not as you remember them; every child develops in his or her own good time. Just be patient, leave it to us, and Johnny will eventually blossom.

When Somers-Beebe asked how long she had to wait for Johnny to blossom, the educators had no answer. When schools become gardens, it's hard to tell who will blossom when, apparently, especially if some parts of the garden receive no water. The educators did promise research on the fertility of the activity centres.[1] They also said they welcomed "parent participation," especially when the parents asked their questions nicely.

In a later meeting with the Peterborough School Board's director of education and the superintendent of curriculum, Somers-Beebe repeated her questions. She was told that only the provincial Ministry of Education could answer her. At another meeting, board administrators told other representatives of Parents for Education (Somers-Beebe had not been allowed to attend because of "hostile body language") that the board would look into a curriculum for elementary education. The superintendent said it might take a year.

To placate Parents for Education, the board then held a "learning symposium" at which experts from other boards tried to answer questions that should have been answered at South Monaghan. Shortly after that, the board reluctantly tested the failing students that so concerned Somers-Beebe and found that twelve of twenty-one children who had attended kindergarten to Grade 4 together were reading at a mid-Grade 2 level. Many couldn't pen complete sentences or even spell words such as "cat" or "him."

No longer able to deny the obvious, the board established an ill-defined remedial program that consisted of reading "Every Time I Climb a Tree," a low-vocabulary high-interest reader — the kind that usually keeps a child's vocabulary small and fails to hold his or her interest. The resource teacher told the parents that, if they wanted direct, sequential instruction, they would "have to go out and pay for it." A teacher's aide actually taught most of the remedial lessons.

In the end, the board said it tried to answer Somers-Beebe's "deceptively simple" questions, noting that South Monaghan staff had "been under severe stress created by the expectations of Parents for Education." During summer break, the principal transferred to another school and half the teaching staff turned over. Somers-Beebe, disgusted by the school's inability to do the right thing, enrolled Adam in a nearby Catholic school. There he was immediately assessed, taken off the activity circuit, and given direct teaching in reading, writing, and math. He now reads at a 7.1 reading level in Grade 5.

Being community-minded, Somers-Beebe also set up a home-tutoring program for seventeen students with Monaghan's two-year-wide learning gaps because, as she noted, the board's "half-assed" remedial program didn't make much of a difference. The parents of three other children opted for home schooling. "We never thought it would get this appalling," Somers-Beebe said, "but morally we couldn't let it go because our children were involved. These people have no respect for parents, and I don't think they care about children either."

DEWEY AND PROGRESSIVISM

The inability of educators to answer Maureen Somers-Beebe's fundamental questions, let alone to teach her children the basics, has become commonplace in North America. This growing ignorance of the rudiments of old-fashioned schooling is neither arbitrary nor incidental. The plight of Maureen Somers-Beebe, and of hundreds of thousands of other parents, represents the overthrow of the school's original mission by sweet-sounding progressive dogma.

Progressivism was largely fathered by John Dewey, an American philosopher whose passion for innovation grew out of his own disagreeable memories of public education. His ideas have gradually turned the school from a traditional place of learning and teaching into a chaotic centre for child care, social engineering, and "relevant" activities. The curriculum, as Somers-Beebe discovered, often stems from the children's own whims.

The most widely regarded educational philosopher since Plato, Dewey was a white, middle-class social scientist. He died in 1952 at the age of ninety-two, but his influence lives on. A father of five, he thought of schools as just one of the many formal social institutions by which adults intentionally pass on culture to the young. He believed that the best education is incidental, as it often appears to be in families, and he advocated that schools become incidental factories of social change. Disheartened by the alienating nature of monopoly capitalism, he and his disciples thought the school could be an effective tool for preparing citizens to "humanize" an economic system not noted for its humanity.

In 1916 Dewey wrote, "The kind of education in which I am interested is not one which will adapt workers to the existing industrial regime; I am not sufficiently in love with the regime for that. It seems to me that the business of all those who would not be educational time servers is to resist every move in this direction, and to strive for a kind of vocational education which will first alter the existing industrial system, and ultimately transform it." In assigning schools such a grand and impossible task, he and his followers unwittingly set in motion a destructive social pendulum. In the last fifty years it has swung from unrealistic expectations for the schools as an instrument of social change to disenchantment with the schools as dull and unsafe places.

To create Utopia, Dewey advocated a new democratic curriculum that addressed "the whole vast panorama of human affairs." He thought the best route to this new body of scientific and industrial studies was "learning by doing" and cherished the notion that the child should become "the sun about which the appliances of education revolve; he is the centre about which they are organized." The teacher was just one of these appliances.

With his overriding faith in science, Dewey reduced schooling to a classroom equation of activity, interest, discovery, and problem solving. Ever since he first wrote about these ideas, however, educators have mistaken his philosophy for a recipe. Indeed, before his death in 1952, Dewey condemned colleagues who pushed the notion of child-centred development to fatuous extremes: "Nothing can be developed from nothing, nothing but the crude can be developed out of the crude, and this is surely what happens when we throw the child back upon his achieved self as a finality, and invite him to spin new truths of nature or of conduct out of that." He also ridiculed progressive schools that deemed "orderly organization of subject-matter hostile to the needs of students."

Like the followers of many secular cults, however, Deweyites did not heed or even read the master. For most of this century the basic tenets of progressivism have been served in the schools like some kind of wonder stew. The spicy buzzwords, then as now, remain self-realization, group integration, economic efficiency, and the primacy of process. Children were no longer to be taught the basics but rather indoctrinated in the stuff of the here and now: "education for life." Children should learn on their own and from their own experiences. Learning is natural, developmental, and fun. The teacher is not a taskmaster or spoon feeder but a guide. He or she should not specialize in subjects but in "the scientific study of pupil development." Teach the whole child, went one clarion call, not the subject.

The progressives argued that school should be fitted to the needs of the individual child in order that society could fit the man or woman for comfortable industrial employment or leisure. "The Guardians of the young," wrote G. Stanley Hall, a Harvard-trained mentor of Dewey's, "should strive first of all to keep out of nature's way and to prevent harm, and should merit the proud titles of defenders of the happiness and rights of children."

In the 1950s, three decades after the founding of the progressive movement, an Alberta functionary wrote that the primary aim of a progressive school was "to develop the social intelligence of the child in order to assist him to come to grips with the social problems of adult living." Children should work at current problems and controversial issues in order to become democrats in "a problem-solving world." The progressive school also championed "experimentalism" and the scientific method because both were "rooted in experience." Learning, after all, "must be related to living."[2]

Over time, progressive educators erased the motto of the populist community school — "Knowledge is power" — and replaced it with a modern half truth: "Activity and growth are power." Such views nicely complemented Dewey's own slogan: "Not knowledge or information, but self-realization, is the goal."

The views of John Dewey and his followers on childhood education developed within a larger progressive vision of society. For most of this century, North America's business, media, and education élites have been progressives in spirit if not in deed. As a professional class in pursuit of happy modernity, they have promoted the desirability and inevitability of technical and economic development, what the American historian Christopher Lasch calls "the promise of steady improvement with no foreseeable ending at all." But when the élites accepted perpetual innovation as the fuel of cultural and economic life, they reduced belief to passing fad, and tradition to outdated information.

Having rejected religious faith as backward and parochial, the progressives embraced a messy moral relativism. If it feels good, the reasoning went, do it, because doing, no matter what the context, is learning. Seeking to free humankind from manual labour, material discomfort, and even the task of nurturing the young, progressives have advocated "the private enjoyment of life." In his critique of the progressive mind, *The True and Only Heaven*, Lasch concluded that progressives loudly rate tolerance as the supreme political virtue while quietly championing narcissism as the model of psychic health.

Decorated with university degrees, the progressives look dismissively at people without degrees. There is no such thing as common sense in the progressive book—only the moral wisdom of technicians who speak in tongues. The most refined progressive of this century has been the young, upwardly mobile professional. Of all North America's institutions, the media and the schools have been most infiltrated by the progressive ethos. There is now a little of the progressive in all of us.

One of the basic tenets of today's progressive education — and one that Dewey clearly did not intend — was an openness to any subject matter. The nineteenth-century school held that a few academic disciplines, such as English, history, and math, were essential, but the new democratic school embraced every topic under the sun. North American educators came to regard any subject, from personal hairstyling to Buddhist philosophy, as an equally effective way of becoming a "self-realized" or "life-adjusted" consumer prepared for a life of social change.

By the 1930s, the graduates of teachers' colleges typically regarded mathematics or ancient languages as misguided avenues to educational growth. They considered subjects such as dancing, dramatics, and doll-playing as the best way to self-realization. To this list, hip educators have added thematic discussions of racism, multiculturalism, gender equity, and global peace.

PRISONERS OF THE GOOD IDEA

This pollution of the school day with often mindless activities has characterized North American elementary schooling for most of this century. Not long after the turn of the century, Agnes Deans Cameron, a teacher in British Columbia, reported that the task of defending the intellectual needs of her pupils for five hours a day had become onerous. Specialists and missionaries of all stripes, she reported, now clamoured for faddish enrichment programs. The Women's Christian Temperance Union wanted to dangle a hob-nailed liver in front of the class. An animal rights group, the Bands of Mercy, wanted to teach children how to love cats and dogs. The British Columbia Council of Women insisted that there be cooking stoves and stew pans on every desk. And government bureaucrats, anxious about farm income, demanded that new immigrants get a course in farming (using Ontario textbooks with information on Ontario soils and Ontario weeds). "You can't open your schoolroom door for a breath of fresh air without letting someone with a mission fall in," Cameron wrote. To her the issue was not whether dickey-bird drawing, cooking, cat-fawning, and straw weaving were good or bad, but this fundamental truth: "Five hours is a period of time with mathematical limitations. You can't crowd something new into it, without crowding something old out.... In the school, as elsewhere in this busy world of emulation, of turmoil and competition, we attempt too much — eagerness takes the place of earnestness; and we are out of touch with the good old-fashioned virtues of thoughtfulness and thoroughness."

Cameron expressed those sentiments in 1904. Ninety years later, the limits of five hours of instruction continue to be stretched by demands from special interest groups calling for AIDS education, self-esteem building, stress reduction, computer literacy, multiculturalism, gay lifestyle programs, environmental awareness, and global thinking. Faced with this ever-growing and infinitely flexible curriculum, a history teacher at a high school in Ottawa recently repeated Cameron's plea by noting that educators are "the prisoners of the good idea. Our problem is not that we do too little, but rather, that we try to do too much....What a paradox. By trying to do more, we end up doing less."

Doing more and achieving less in school is a peculiarly North American endeavour, and its effects are more remarkable and immediate than most people realize. As the English novelist and social critic Aldous Huxley noted three decades ago in his essay "Knowledge and Understanding," progressivism put the United States (and, at a slower pace, Canada) on a course opposite to that of the rest of the world. While Europe and Asia strove to impart more basic knowledge to their students, North America seemingly aimed for total idiocy. Before World War I, for example, 56 per cent of all American high school students took algebra; after World War II, that number had fallen to 25 per cent. In geometry, the percentage fell from 27 to 11. With progressivism, wrote Huxley in the 1950s, came "doing without learning, along with courses in adjustment to everything except the basic twentieth-century fact that we live in a world where ignorance of science and its methods is the surest, shortest road to national disaster." Any society that abandoned the populist notion that "learning, by any method, must always be hard work," he predicted, would find itself in full decline within a generation or two. In North America, that prediction has been borne out.

Under the aegis of progressivism, North American high schools from Newfoundland to California became what has been called "supermarkets for educational merchandise." Before the 1920s, the typical high school offered no more than twenty-four academic courses. By World War II, subject matter had multiplied like Australia's rabbits to include more than three hundred items, of which only about a third could claim any academic content. Today some Canadian and American school boards offer as many as seven hundred study items. The product line has evolved from unglamorous items such as Family Living, Consumer Economics, and Job Information to the fashionably hip: Shopping and Community

Resources, Behaviour and Society, Marriage Simulation, Gourmet Cuisine, and Baja Whalewatch. Some high schools have even set up classes in shopping malls.[3]

This manifestly anti-intellectual curriculum is often lauded as being superior to an academic one because of its relevance, fairness, and air of democracy. Defenders of the supermarket curriculum argue that it allows schools to respond differentially to the differing needs of students by streaming more youngsters into hairstyling than into history or physics. As the American historian Richard Hofstadter points out, however, this peculiar vision of democracy, now held by most educational administrators, made it possible for schools "to assert that immature, insecure, nervous, retarded slow learners from poor cultural environments were 'in no sense inferior' to more mature, secure, confident, gifted children from better cultural environments. This verbal genuflection before 'democracy' seems to have enabled them to conceal from themselves that they were, with breathtaking certainty, writing off the majority of the nation's children as being more or less uneducable." Neither Japan nor Europe chose to emulate this elaborate and systematic form of discrimination against working people.[4]

The full weight of progressive dogma did not really fall upon Canadian schools until the 1960s. Although the Canadian prairie feminist and nationalist Hilda Neatby identified the progressive takeover of Canadian educational policy in her 1953 bestseller, *So Little for the Mind*, classroom practices remained a combination of the traditional, the effective, and the dull. She predicted, however, that Deweyite curricula designed to cater to children's interests not only would create bored "self-centred little automatons" but would eventually destroy the school with intellectual barbarism and moral anarchy. A true education, she believed, entailed the discovery that the world is more interesting than oneself. And she saw the child-centred school as a dangerous innovation because "it does not express the belief that the world, or rather ideas, which are generalizations about the world, are really very interesting." In response to the progressive dictum "Remember, you're not teaching English, you're teaching the child," she retorted: "Pour me a cup of coffee and remember you're not pouring coffee, you're pouring me."

In the late 1960s, two pivotal educational documents, the Plowden Report in England and the Hall-Dennis Report in Ontario, embraced child-centred education as the only correct future for public schools. Both documents were written largely by white, upper-middle-class liberals; both praised Dewey and his interpreters in self-righteous, ideological prose. Both urged that children should go to school to learn more about children. The Plowden Report concludes, "A school is not merely a teaching shop, it must transmit values and attitudes. It is a community in which children learn to live first and foremost as children and not as future adults. In family life children learn to live with people of all ages. The school sets out deliberately to devise the right environment for children, to allow them to be themselves and to develop in the way and at the pace appropriate to them.... It lays special stress on individual discovery, on first-hand experience and on opportunities for creative work...."

The Hall-Dennis Report was full of similar progressive slogans. "Learning is by its very nature a personal matter." "Learning should be dynamic." "Children are the focus of attention and the atmosphere within the classroom must be positive and encouraging." And so forth. In a critique of the report, Robin Barrow, a professor of education in Canada, wonders who ever argued that classrooms should be negative and discouraging, or that learning should be undynamic, or that chairs instead of students should be the focus of attention. Learning is indeed personal, of course, in the sense that one student cannot learn for another, but Hall-Dennis entertained farce by suggesting that only chance and the child can determine what is learned.

Both documents dismissed the school as a place for intellectual training, cultural enlightenment, or moral instruction; they breezily advocated doing away with grades and standards. With the age of doing came the age of relativism.[5]

A TYPICAL SCHOOL

Let's visit, for a moment, a Grade 4 classroom near Toronto in a school on the cutting edge of progressive, child-centred pedagogy. It is nine o'clock in the morning. Five minutes pass before the twenty-two students find their seats at four sets of tables grouped to form rectangles. Because of this arrangement, only half the class can see the teacher at any time.

The classroom itself looks like an advertisement for a holiday in Brazil. From the ceiling hang large cardboard posters of violins, trumpets, and drums. Red, yellow, and green coloured paper plasters the walls. Pictures, drawings, maps, diagrams, rules, math problems, word families, hockey players, animal skins, cartoons, and puzzles all compete for the eye. Books, papers, and boxes of sundry articles lie heaped on tables. One blank green three-by-five-foot space on a wall appears to be a chalkboard.

With little fanfare or sense of beginnings, the teacher presents a lesson about the differences between fruits and vegetables, the prices of fruits and vegetables, why cooks and botanists don't agree about the classification of fruits and vegetables, and what parts of fruits and vegetables one should eat. As the teacher talks, the students write down the names of bananas and apples and their price. They write with crayons, pens, pencils, and Magic Markers; they write on lined paper, plain paper, scrap paper, and photocopied forms. One or two students write on their desks. The teacher stops for a moment to encourage several students not to play with Plasticine while working with their calculators.

The lesson is part of a week-long project to prepare a dinner for school staff: learning by doing. Math, reading, and writing have been abandoned in favour of grocery shopping and vegetable pricing. Last month a music project had pre-empted reading; the month before that math had been sacrificed to an activity involving animal skins. The teacher, it appeared, changed subjects as whimsically as people flick through television channels.

Learning by doing has demonstrable limits, but educators haven't yet grasped them. At one point in the 1980s, well-funded middle-class high schools across North America taught concepts by presenting them as disjointed concrete blocks that belong to no greater building. In New York, Leonard Peikoff, an American philosopher and associate of Ayn Rand, visited several high schools and found nine- and ten-year-olds discussing the thirteen steps for hunting seals, beginning with hole cutting and ending with blubber eating. (No members of the class were Inuit or Eskimo.) In another class, thirteen-year-olds re-enacted a Washington hearing on whether to tax imported Japanese cars. And in an English class (the observer couldn't figure out what subject the other classes were ostensibly concerned with), students were reading Robert Kennedy's *Thirteen Days*, a hastily written memoir of the Cuban missile crisis.

The school defended this subject matter as relevant, child-centred, and democratic, but the observer was mystified by "the anti-conceptual approach.... Seal hunting was not used to illustrate the rigors of Northern life or the method of analyzing a skill into steps or anything at all. The issue of taxing Japanese cars was not related to a study of free trade verus protectionism or of the proper function of government, or of the principles of foreign policy or any principles." In every case something concrete was being taught, debated, and argued. But could it be that, in every case, perceiving was mistaken for thinking?

THE DUMBING OF TEXTS

The anti-intellectualism of progressive thought has found ample expression in the dumbing of school texts. A century and a half ago, school readers such as McGuffey's began at a certain level of difficulty and gradually employed a more challenging vocabulary. Reason and continuity no longer exist in primary readers. A New

Jersey sociologist recently measured this free fall into literal stupidity by devising a lexical scale to measure the frequency of common and uncommon words in a variety of reading matter.[6] On this scale, a magazine such as *Physics Today* scores 13, newpapers 0, and comic books -26. In reviewing first-grade readers over a 130-year period, the reseacher found that basal readers had become simpler if not more simple-minded than comic books; they scored -64. To the researcher's surprise, the score remained constant for the entire Grade 1 reader. Basal readers that, in the 1920s, contained 645 different words now average a count of 350 words or fewer. Publishers such as Ginn, Scott Foresmen, and Houghton Mifflin now compose beginning readers with the same kind of language that farmers use to talk to cows.

Along with the humiliation of the word has come a new reverence for pictures. The average Grade 1 book now contains two or three times as many illustrations or drawings as it did sixty years ago. By telling more of the story, pictures inevitably take away the incentive to read. The research about such visual methods is plain. Books with pictures teach children how to interpret pictures; books with words teach children how to read.

The pictures in modern-day readers not only eschew the hard and rewarding work of learning but undermine the very act of reading. They commonly portray children as idiots who do little more than play with animals (cats, dogs, turtles, frogs) or anxiously await surprises such as a colour TV. School often appears in these instructional books as a place to escape from, or as a setting for fun activities such as painting or puppet making. One of North America's most popular reading series, Impressions, instructs children to stay up late, follow their own bedtime rules, "ask to watch one more television show," and then "dream wonderful dreams about not going to bed." Such attacks on reading, let alone on family culture, imply, as the great child psychologist Bruno Bettelheim once observed, that "school and learning are so unattractive that the only way to induce a child to go to school is by providing him with enjoyable nonacademic events in the classroom."

The debasement of school readers reflects the triumph of one particular approach to the teaching of reading. Alternatively called "look-say," "language experience," "psycholinguistics," and, most recently, "whole language," this method teaches children to guess words by context, initial letter, or picture clues. Because reading is supposed to be more meaningful this way, it is often called the "meaning approach" to reading.[7]

The reading-for-meaning movement stems from Jean-Jacques Rousseau's nineteenth-century idea that man should study wholes, not parts. When the idea was first applied to reading, in the 1870s, educators invented the look-and-say method. The chief spokesman for look-and-say was the American psychologist Edmund Huey. In 1908 he wrote that "the golden years of child-hood" belong to pursuits other than reading and writing. Those subjects, he maintained, shouldn't begin until a child is nine. Reading "should always be for the intrinsic meaning of what is read." Start with the whole — sentence meanings first — and for-get the rest. Huey based his observations on the reading habits of a few upper-class Boston children. To John Dewey, who knew little about the pedagogy of reading, memorizing whole words sounded a lot like learning by doing. In the wake of Huey and Dewey came Dick and Jane, Mr. Mugs, and Impressions. Phonics, which had dominated reading instruction for three thousand years, was con-signed to the dustbin.

The teacher manuals of the reading-for-meaning series begin and end with preposterous statements. Ginn's 1969 manual, for example, tells teachers that "children should be given every oppor-tunity to think and reason. From the first story in the pre-primer, the pupils are required to interpret the pictures, size up the situa-tions and formulate their own purposes for reading." Nelson's 1977 resource book advises teachers that reading is "a psycholin-guistic process in which the reader interacts with print to get meaning." Skill development proceeds from units of meaning (whole studies) to smaller units (paragraphs, sentences, and word parts). This top-to-bottom approach "should assist children in confirming their insights about getting meaning from print." The Impressions series advises teachers that reading is "a meaning-seeking process" in which children use their own language and experiences as "a major resource." All these manuals perpetuate the myth that learning to read is really the child's responsibility because learning to read is as natural as learning to speak. In fact, neither history nor science supports this institutionalized confusion of speech (a biological activity) with script (a learned artefact).

Contrast the obfuscation of the whole language readers with the stated purpose of Open Court, an acclaimed phonics series: "To teach children to read and write independently by the end of the first grade."[8] To achieve this end, the Grade I readers introduce forty-one sounds, four sound combinations, and 2,326 words in the context of nursery rhymes, fables, and fairy tales. No televisions and very few pictures appear in this series. In most North American jurisdictions, progressive educators have banned Open Court readers as unnatural and unwholesome.

In the spring of 1988, the *Whole Language Teachers Newsletter* offered this advice to teachers if a student stumbled upon an unknown word: "Foremost on the list of Don'ts are sound-it-out and look-for-familiar-word parts within the word because these activities divert the reader's attention from meaning.... Good things to do include skip it, use prior information...read ahead, re-read, or put in another word that makes sense."

As a reading strategy, skipping or guessing is one of the biggest frauds ever perpetrated in the classroom. It has meant that students in Grade 3 can't accurately read "A boy said, 'Run little girl.'" Equipped only to guess, they translate the sentence as anything from "A baby is running little go" to "A bird says, 'Run little guy'" or any of a hundred other risk-taking variations. In the meaning approach, detail and distinction, the hallmarks of a literate culture, simply don't count.

THE IMAGE AND THE WORD

The dominance of the word-recognition or meaning approach in North American schools merely signals the larger triumph of the image over the word. As computers, television, and audio-visual aids have become an increasingly common medium of classroom instruction, it's perhaps not surprising that educators would expect children to recognize words the way they would a picture of a sports hero or a popular cereal. Word guessing or look-say simply mimics audio-visual learning; it leads students "as spectators," in the words of Jacques Ellul, "directly to a result." Ellul, a French critic of modern technological society, points out that, when the efficient gratification of the visual senses becomes the purpose of reading instruction, the analysis of words and sounds falls into disrepute.

Few teachers recognize their slavish employment of images as not only an assault on literacy but also a war on any ideas that cannot be communicated by ideographs. The almost uncritical acceptance of visual presentations in North American classrooms has meant a complete disregard for the paralytic effect of images on youthful thought. Learning by sight, like learning by doing, may be useful and efficient, but it systematically discourages thinking (a step-by-step process linked to mastery of reading and writing) and erases memory. It invites conformity to a universe of common images and it places an individual forever in a world of spectacular-looking things rather than of great ideas. By imparting little depth, the pedagogical image also imprisons students in the immediate, and in their own private being. Ultimately, Ellul argues, a classroom driven by films, computers, posters, and image-dominant books teaches a child three fundamental lies: that "everything is possible, that everything is always new, and that circumstances are so fluid that he can influence or master them."

The flood of images that has diluted reading classes and overpowered instruction, he believes, heralds another evil: "We forget all too easily that imagination is the basic characteristic of intelligence, so that a society in which people lose their capacity to conjure up symbols also loses its inventiveness and its ability to act."

As schools have increased their reliance on images and audio-visual techniques, literacy levels have naturally fallen. This decline signals the serious conflict between two competing forms of educational thinking: the progressive, which relies on image and intuition, and the traditional, which involves disciplined thought with words. This intellectual battle is ironically underscored every time progressive teachers reluctantly assess a student's ability to express written ideas clearly. "Pupils take in images, and we require that they respond with discourse," notes Ellul. "Switching from one to the other is impossible." The resistance of educators to clear and literate evaluations of student performance surely reflects an unconscious allegiance to the new pedagogical king: learning by sight.

THE ABANDONMENT OF LITERACY

The results of the sight-driven reading curriculum now used in schools throughout North America are predictable enough. Between 20 and 25 per cent of all white middle-class school children no longer learn how to read very well in school. The percentages for children of poverty are much higher. In black and Hispanic neighbourhoods of New York City, 70 per cent of all ninth graders read below their grade level, which means that most books and even magazines are beyond their reach or interest.

In Canada the number of poor readers grows as inexorably as the national debt. A 1987 Southam poll found that 24 per cent of young Canadians could not read well and that 17 per cent of high school graduates were functionally illiterate. A 1989 survey of literacy skills by Statistics Canada reported even grimmer news: almost a third of Canadian high school graduates could not meet everyday reading demands. Another 38 per cent found it difficult to write a note asking a member of their household to repair the oven. Alarming as these studies are, they don't even begin to record what is being lost in reasoning power.

The great American educator Jacques Barzun calls this abandonment of literacy a form of preposterism, the belief that worthy ends can be achieved without hard-working beginnings. Flouting the alphabet — eschewing the struggle of sounding things out — may have freed children's spirits and given bohemian reign to self-expression, but it has not created people who read books and cherish the power of the word. "The causes are not ignorance, poverty or barbarous instincts; they are 'advanced thinking,' love of liberty, and the impulse to discover and innovate. It is from on top — by the action of the literate, the cultured, the philosophical, the artistic — that the common faith in the power of reading as central to western civilization has been destroyed."

WRITING BY DOING

Advanced thinking has also thwarted the teaching of writing. Although the old "hammer the grammar" school produced dubious results, progressives have merely replaced one poor method with another: writing by doing. To the progressive educator, writing is as natural as reading, which is as natural as walking, and having students write about anything but themselves would be highly unnatural. Many schools have reduced writing to the keeping of personal journals in which students "discover" themselves or "explore a subject." Directed mostly to an audience of peers, and full of "invented spelling," these journals are rarely corrected. One of the gurus of the so-called "natural process mode" notes, "Writing is learned by doing it and sharing it with real audiences, not by studying and applying abstract rhetorical principles in exercises which the teacher alone will read and judge."

In this natural approach, a teacher is often forbidden to assign specific writing topics, help students learn criteria for judging excellent and clear prose, or structure lessons around specific objectives, such as the presentation of an argument. The research suggests that this free-writing approach is only marginally more effective than beating nouns and verbs into a student's brain. With its emphasis on self-interest, writing by doing often forbids a teacher to uphold the literary tradition, for only by reading and writing about good works of literature and journalism will a student become a fine writer. "However much a new writer may have to say," wrote the great critic Northrop Frye, "his ability to say it can only be developed out of his reading; in other words it will depend on his scholarship."

In the modern school, writing has become just another playful activity that more closely resembles masturbation than the thoughtful application of language in a complex or extended fashion. Grammar, a critical tool for writing and thinking, is no longer a part of most school curricula. The natural approach may increase fluency, but it is largely a recipe for graduating self-centred scribblers who misspell much of what they may have discovered. Universities and community colleges across the continent now report that as many as a third of their students cannot compose coherent sentences or paragraphs using standard English spelling. One in three college-bound students in Ontario fashions free-form English that would make George Orwell wince. A high school graduate recently wrote on an entrance exam: "The misapprehension of the language structure used in society has often lead to its destruction." When the U.S. Educational Testing Service asked several thousand seventeen-year-olds to write a convincing letter to get a summer job at a swimming pool, nearly a quarter replied with one sentence: "I want to work in the pool." Half the students elaborated with invented spellings. Here's a typical response: "I have been experience at cleaning house. Ive also work at a pool be for. I love keeping things neat organized and clean. Im very social I'll get to know peopl really fast. I never forget to do things."

Schools, of course, merely reflect society's decreasing regard for written language and thought. Much of the written language citizens now encounter at work and at home is bureaucratic or legal-minded. Polluted by cliché, burdened by the demands of promotion, advertising, and corporate self-justification, much written language — whether on mortgage applications, tax returns, or report cards — appears distant, unbelievable, and uncommon. Warnings and bad news tend to arrive in printed form, as Leon Botstein noted recently in the literary journal *Daedalus*, while good news makes the telephone ring. Businessmen, lawyers, and academics purposely use jargon and a technical vocabulary that have the ultimate effect of shielding the content of their writing from widespread scrutiny.

Gradually, the social motivation to master the written acts of thinking and remembering is being erased. At the same time, the things that many North Americans prize most, such as the freedom to order pizza at four o'clock in the morning, bear little relationship to knowledge of the written word. Instead of challenging these social trends and defending the word, educational administrators now support what Botstein calls a "severely crippled and limited form of literacy."

SCIENCE IS HAPPENING HERE

Not long ago Josef Macek, a Czech-born geologist who emigrated to Canada in 1969, became alarmed at the absence of basic physics and chemistry classes in Manitoba's high school science program. The existing curriculum was then and remains a patchwork of American guidelines and American texts replete with cartoons. Eager to understand why his sons were not learning any basic science at school, he compared Manitoba's science curricula to those of his homeland. He found that Grade 7 students in Czechoslovakia knew more basic science than Grade 10 students in Manitoba. He also found that the Czech program consisted of nothing more than logically designed textbooks that present an incremental build-up of knowledge geared towards educating average-ability students from the working class. The Czech students came from crowded and polluted neighbourhoods where both parents typically worked and families shared small apartments. At the Czech schools, the average class size ranged from thirty to forty students.

In contrast, Manitoba's science program consisted of a "smorgasbord of material" vaguely aimed at raising "science appreciation" rather than building knowledge. Manitoba sought to achieve this end by asking students to observe a burning candle one day and to inflate balloons, collide marbles, plant beans, or discuss changes in the weather the next. Equipped with little more than cartoon texts and laconic suggestions from wordy guidelines, Manitoba teachers faced the unreal task of trying somehow to relate bean growing to marble colliding. Asking teachers to make sense of such a curricular mess, wrote Macek, was equivalent to "equipping a dentist with a pair of pliers, a chisel and a hammer, and expecting him to perform fine bridge work."[9]

In a recent study of North American textbooks, Harriet Tyson-Bernstein, an American researcher, concluded, as had Macek, that they offered nothing more than a "thin stream of staccato prose winding through an excessive number of pictures, boxes, and charts." In their quest for dollars, educational publishers have attempted to please the greatest number of school boards by mentioning as many sellable facts, people, and events as could be crammed into one book.

Textbooks designed for the visual senses may not be difficult to read but often make no sense. One Canadian science writer recently confessed in a letter to Josef Macek that it is frustrating as a writer "to rationalize vague curricula that often seem to have been created by groups of people sitting around a table throwing out their pet ideas and topics. There is often no obvious sequence or even coherence among the bits and pieces of knowledge that constitute a set of required learning outcomes. In addition curricula and text organization and style are dictated by pedagogical consultants and civil servants who are often, in my experience, fairly ignorant about science and much else. As for textbooks being useful references and sources of concrete data, you have to go back twenty years to find those. Everything is now process and fad."

A recent comparison of Canadian school texts — in math, physics, and chemistry — with the equivalent Japanese and German texts illustrated some mighty differences between child-centred learning, using images, and mind-centred learning, using words.[10] Compared to Japan's inexpensive paperbacks and Germany's concise concept presentations, Canadian textbooks were thicker, costlier, and more cartoon-laden. In the Canadian primers, concepts were repeated gratuitously, introduced much later in the school term, and seemed to assume a lack of rapport between teacher and student.

Overall, however, the basic curriculum did not differ all that much from one country to another. The researchers concluded that the superior performance of Japanese and German students on international achievement tests in these subjects "probably lies in superior education practices and perhaps cultural differences." Unlike Japan and Germany, the researchers believed, North America had drifted towards "self-discovery, individualism, sensual indulgence, pursuit of personal happiness and self-fulfillment."

In 1985 the noted physicist Richard Feynman served on the California State Board of Education Textbook Commission. Its decisions, along with those of the Texas board, influence the purchasing habits of most other school jurisdictions on the continent; what goes around in California often comes around to the rest of North America's schools. As a commission member, Feynman was called upon to review a math textbook with blank pages, which a publisher had submitted by accident. To Feynman's horror, six of his fellow commission members rated the book "above average."

Few documents illustrate the vapidity of science instruction in the elementary grades as well as Ontario's *Science Is Happening Here*. This forty-seven-page guide offers no sense of continuity, of one step building to another; rather, it's a random dramatization of individual experiences ("learning opportunities") with energy, water, space, growth, and matter. It confuses the study of technologies that make middle-class homes comfortable ("becoming aware of toothbrushes, freezers and steam irons") with science as a structured way of thinking about particular living or inanimate objects. When not "gathering information using a variety of communication techniques," students are invited to recognize "that they are doing science." The authors of this travesty were probably influenced by "Creative Sciencing," the work of two professors at Purdue University. Designed to tell science teachers how to teach, this text recommends "lots of hands-on activities" from bug catching to star gazing in no particular order. It also says that truth doesn't matter: "When preparing performance objectives," recommends the book's authors, "you may wish to consider the fact that we don't demand accuracy in art or creative writing, but we have permitted ourselves to require accuracy in science. We may be paying a high price in lost interest, enthusiasm, vitality, and creativity in science because of this requirement of accuracy."

Not long ago, when Toronto sociologist Dennis Raphael explained why this vague, child-centred curriculum yielded low science achievement scores, a teacher in the audience made a predictable admission. "If students enjoyed working with science-type materials such as magnets or mirrors, I really don't care if they learned anything." A principal standing nearby added, "As an educator, I fully agree with that view. As a parent, it scares me to death."

Now that science textbooks have become glorified scrapbooks and school work has turned into a succession of pleasing activities with no more depth than a television sitcom, perhaps the most disturbing thing of all is society's tolerance of the educationally intolerable. "It is odd that in an age when the word 'context' is continually used as a reminder of the way things hang together," writes Jacques Barzun, "that people should have tolerated schools where context is hourly destroyed."

SPIRALLING NUMBERS

The progressive follies so evident in the modern approach to reading and writing have also transformed mathematics instruction. Early in the century, math got caught in an ideological debate between traditionalists and the adding-for-meaning crowd. This futile debate has had a futile outcome: math teaching is now actually fixed in a maddening spiral curriculum that repeats topics *ad nauseam* from year to year.

The spiral curriculum came into vogue in the 1970s after the New Math — a short-lived experimental program that stressed meaning rather than computing — became old. It's based on the idea that mathematical ideas are as simple as they are powerful. To master them, a student need only apply these ideas in progressively more complex forms over time. When translated into a curriculum, however, this idea became a parade of endless math topics, repeated year after year. Students may work on geometry for two weeks and then drop it and go on to fractions. The great lesson learned in this approach is that nothing is important because it disappears. And if nothing is important, why master it? The ugly consequence of all this spiralling is that the same vague and familiar goals linger like ghosts, never taking logical shape in children's minds.[11]

The International Assocation for the Evaluation of Educational Achievement, a semi-private agency funded by both governments and corporations, highlighted the stupidity of this system in 1987 when it reported that only 40 per cent of Grade 8 students in the United States could add two-fifths and one-eighth, even though they had pursued fractions on a spiral staircase since Grade I. More teaching of fractions increased the percentage of achievers at the end of Grade 8 by less than 20 per cent. In other words, four of five pupils merely repeated what they had already learned. In France, by contrast, where students aren't served a math smorgasbord in elementary school, only one in twenty could perform the addition at the beginning of Grade 8. But after intense and thorough coverage of the subject, 73 per cent had mastered the concept by year's end. In France, more than two-thirds of the math class actually learned something.

The spiral curriculum becomes ever more dizzying when combined with the latest fad: "discovery math." Jeff Martin, the co-ordinator of mathematics for the Etobicoke Board of Education in Ontario, recently defined the merits of this natural approach: "Who does the child's learning for them? Is it the national curriculum? Is it the teacher, the supervisor?... No, the child does his/her own learning for themselves (sic). If we want to know how kids learn then we need to watch them, ask them thought-provoking questions, involve them collaboratively in the discovery. Mathematics is all about children making discoveries about patterns and structures and using these discoveries to discover more mathematics.... If we believe, and rightly so, in a learner-centred environment, that children possess the natural ability to think, then by questioning, letting children argue, encouraging them to reinvent their own methods of arithmetic, then it is necessary to provide rich mathematical experiences with kids communicating reasoning and seeing connections with the real world."

Taken to its logical extreme, Martin's views imply a curriculum that would have students searching for the Pythagorean theorem until they reached the age of senility, still unsatisfied in their personal quest to discover what is already known.

The "let-them-discover-math" approach has left a lot of children thinking they have arrived someplace when in fact they have never left home. In 1989 the Second International Mathematics

Study National Assessment of Educational Progress reported that only 16 per cent of America's Grade 8 students had mastered the content of a typical eighth-grade mathematics textbook. Even at that, the definition of mastery was less than rigorous — successful students were those who could compute with decimals, fractions, and percentages, and solve simple equations, with at least 65 per cent accuracy. The vast majority of students who took the test couldn't perform any of these mathematical tasks with 50 per cent accuracy.

A 1989 international study that compared the math performance of thirteen-year-olds in Korea, Spain, the United States, the United Kingdom, Ireland, and four Canadian provinces also illustrated another fallacy of discovery learning. Students from the United States had the lowest average scores, yet the majority (58 per cent) boasted they were good in math. The Koreans, who ranked highest, didn't suffer from such inflated beliefs: only 28 per cent claimed to be good at numbers.[12]

A similar 1992 study (the International Assessment of Educational Progress II) — it, too, compared the math abilities of thirteen-year-olds in twenty countries — also placed American students near the bottom of the list with an average of 55 per cent. The province of Ontario, Canada's largest, faired only marginally better, scoring 58 per cent and ranking just ahead of Slovenia.

In a recent essay on the waste of educational resources in math teaching, Ed Barbeau, a math professor at the University of Toronto, identified three culprits: bad ideologies that cherish pet theories about children more than learning; a curriculum that has spiralled out of control into a sterile wasteland of unrelated mechanical techniques; and an inability to evaluate student performance fairly or sensibly. "Every generation complains about the standards of education imposed upon its children," Barbeau concluded. "Allowing for this, I and many of my colleagues look upon our current classes and perceive that something is seriously wrong. A student who was failing a generation ago often was able to do something about his failure; he understood why the failure occurred and had enough basic background to build on for a successful second try. What is poignant about many of the present generation of students is that failure comes to them out of the blue at a late stage in their schooling. They have been the victims of a conspiracy to shield them from any knowledge of their inadequacies until these have become so pervasive as to make any remedy of their condition impossible."

CLARIFYING CHARACTER

Long before reading and adding became discovery activities, schools taught moral character. But learning courage, honesty, and generosity by example and practice lost favour in the late 1960s with the rise of decision making, moral reasoning, or discover-your-own-values. Influenced by the theories of California-based psychotherapists such as Carl Rogers and Abraham Maslow, this educational shift complemented child-centred teaching like chalk on chalkboard. Although the new approach claimed to help students think more critically about values, it effectively transformed the Ten Commandments into the Ten Suggestions and thereby produced a new kind of student, one who could justify any kind of behaviour with a snappy one-liner.

The basic premise behind this kind of emotional training is that children should be allowed to choose their own values in the context of group-therapy-like sessions. In such environments, opinions on cannibalism, sex, and wife swapping bounce back and forth like tennis balls, teachers act like Geraldo Rivera and students learn that nothing matters and everything goes. Not surprisingly, the values ultimately chosen belong to the most persuasive and charismatic students of the group. Before Rogers and Maslow died, they both recanted the application of such techniques with children. Educators, however, continue the experiments because "they feel right."

One of the more popular instructional programs in moral relativism is Values Clarification. It encourages children to "tell where [they] stand on the topic of masturbation" and asks, "Whom would you tell you had once taken money from your dad's dresser?" In addition to the program's blatant invasion of privacy, it achieves its narcissistic ends very ably. After clarifying values among his peers, one Toronto high school student wrote, "Moral values cannot be taught and people must learn to use what works for them. In other words, 'whatever gets you through the night, it's alright.' The essence of civilization is not moral codes but individualism....The only way to know when your values are getting sounder is when they please you more."[13]

This kind of nonjudgemental decision-making thinking has also shaped sex education and drug education programs in many schools. The pick-your-own-values approach to drugs and sex, however, results in one powerful achievement: there has been no decrease in sex or drug usage among teenagers. In 1986 Planned Parenthood published the results of two studies that clearly showed no reduction in sexual activity among young women taking sex education courses.[14] Similar studies on a feel-good "affective" drug program called Decide found that those who were encouraged to make choices predictably chose more alcohol, tobacco, and marijuana than controls without such encouragement. Quest, another values clarification drug program, now being offered to 2 million North American students, has yielded similar results. Students who didn't join Quest simply stayed away from cocaine and alcohol in greater numbers than its graduates. "By withholding culture from a whole generation of youth," writes the American Catholic educator William Kilpatrick in *Why Johnny Can't Tell Right From Wrong*, "we are not helping them to 'think for themselves' but only forcing them to patch together crude codes of behavior from the bits and pieces they pick up on television or in the streets."

ALMIGHTY RELEVANCE

Perhaps no word is more important in the progressive school lexicon than relevance. In its name, educators have justified the dismemberment of science into playful activities, and the transformation of history into "contemporary studies" or "conceptual ideas." And in the name of relevance, film strips, television, and computers have replaced books, book learning, and writing.

This obsession with relevance reflects society's dangerous addiction to the immediately useful and its growing ignorance of, if not disdain for, history. Northrop Frye liked to say that relevance was a popular slogan of the Nazis. They talked about *Fachwissenschaft*, or target knowledge, which came to mean the facts and ideas necessary for waging war. In North American education, relevance has come to mean the sights and sounds necessary to "adjust life" to the dynamic processes of consuming in a technological society.

To Frye and most parents, the modern agenda is a denial of the very purpose of education: to develop the intellect and the imagination. This cannot be achieved by offering an ever-changing television-style program of fleeting relevancies and trivia, whether it be transcendental meditation or the reading of *Playboy* magazine (an actual course in one Toronto high school). "It is not the relation of education to the world that matters, it is the relation of the world to education," wrote Frye. In other words, every classroom activity cannot be an existential experience or a sensory bonanza. What matters in learning takes practice and the things that take practice — reading and writing and mathematics — are decreasingly valued in a society married to the relevant moment or image.[15]

Progressive education has taken the idea of public schooling and turned it into an electronic and narcissistic industry where ends are eternally confused with beginnings. In the modern classroom, information poses as knowledge, images as ideas, attention as concentration, activities as continuity, and emotion as truth. Students no longer learn about the realities of human society (knowledge, memory, imagination); instead, they steep themselves in the appearances of a technological society (images, immediacy, sensation) in which the present changes and dissolves like the nightly news.

The result, as Frye observed a decade ago, is neither democratic nor socially desirable: "The young student needs to be protected from society, protected by literature against the flood of imaginative trash that pours into him from the mass media, protected by science against a fascination with gadgets and gimmicks, protected by social science against snobbery and complacency. The crisis of his education comes when he is ready to attach himself to the standards represented by his education, detach himself from his society, and live in the latter as a responsible and critical citizen. If he fails to do this, he will remain a prisoner of his society, unable to break its chains of cliché and prejudice, unable to see through its illusions of advertising and slanted news, unable to distinguish its temporary conventions from the laws of God and man, a spiritual totalitarian. Whether he has voluntarily imprisoned himself or whether he has been betrayed by educators under the pretext of adjusting or 'orienting' him, he cannot live freely or think freely, but is pinioned like Prometheus on his rock."

North America has created a school system that produces dramatic social results, but not the kind any true democrat could admire. Schools that spend most of the day "educating for living" — encouraging students to think about global peace, media literacy, and values clarification — engender predictably idiotic results.

CHAPTER 3

What Went Wrong?
The Great Divorce

"If, as estimated, many children spend thirty hours a week in front of the screen and neglect homework (supposing they are given any), it is because parents are indifferent or feel powerless, but also because they have no clear idea of what a school can and should do. They are, after all, the products of that same, ineffectual, incoherent schooling."   JACQUES BARZUN

CONSPIRACY OF THE LEAST

When North Americans lived where they worked, schools were places that helped local life remain aware of itself. As the Faustian promise of upward mobility took citizens away from their roots, however, the school ceased to be a centre for local life. Much of North America now suffers from two related educational crises: disintegrating communities with no common purpose other than basic survival, and fragmented schools with no sense of place.[1]

Visit, for example, this composite of a typical New York high school, drawn from a 1990 Rand Corporation study of eight schools in the Bronx, Brooklyn, and Manhattan. Half of its two thousand students are black and the other half mainly Hispanic. The majority function at a level two years below their grade and have no hope of reaching any common standard except one based on relativity. Another 12 per cent of the students idle away the hours in special education classes. Most pupils carry knives to school. Some carry guns. Violence against teachers or students can erupt anywhere, any time.

The ostensible mission of the school is solid academic training; in reality, of course, that goal disappeared long ago. The principal, well-meaning and amiable, now tries to meet every new social need with whatever social program he can snare. The school provides parenting classes, attendance outreach, ethnic music, even temporary housing for homeless students. "We couldn't simplify the school," he says, "without neglecting or discriminating against someone." So, day by day, the school becomes more Baroque in its endeavours.

The teachers are mainly Jewish or Irish. About the only thing they share is the parking lot. None of the staff members lives in the community. Each teacher clings to his or her own special program or class, whether it be AIDS awareness or the student newspaper, as if were a life raft. The honest among them admit that they are part of no larger goal than surviving from nine to five within a concrete box.

In this bleak place, the teachers and students have formed a unique and entirely North American social compact, what Theodore Sizer calls a "conspiracy of the least." Teachers demand and expect little mental work (a homework assignment might be to write two sentences about a book being read), and students agree in return not to cause too much trouble. During class the students eat, listen to their Walkmans, and amble around. The school has taught its denizens that doing a bare minimum will yield a diploma. When little is asked, little is given.

Now enter another school, a nearby Catholic enterprise. It has seven hundred poor and disadvantaged pupils from black, Hispanic, and white neighbourhoods. Unlike its public counterpart, this place has an unwavering mission: to produce graduates who are "spiritual, educated, mature, independent, and socially responsible."

Discipline is fair and consistent. Students respect the dress code and the authority vested in the teachers. "When they say something," say the students, "they mean it."

The staff, mostly Catholic lay teachers of all ages, have dedicated themselves to the school's mission. They regard giving up on any student as a personal failure. Many act as counsellors. If a student needs to talk, the teacher steps in; the pupil is not referred to a professional listener.

The curriculum provides a limited menu intended to guarantee students the broadest possible choice after school. There are no electives; everyone is expected to master English, math, science, art, social studies, and physical education. The teaching is sometimes dull and inflexible. Homework is not only assigned but corrected.

The school maintains a sense of tradition. There is a strong feeling among staff that they have a responsibility not only to a generation of students and parents but to the past and future of Catholic schools. Managed on site, the school has achieved a rare and special unity of purpose.

These two schools, which could just as easily be located in Montreal, Los Angeles, or the north end of Winnipeg, owe their divergent cultures to two basic differences. The New York public school now struggles under a central bureaucracy of 4,800 non-teaching staff; the Catholic school, also part of the twelfth largest school system in the United States, reports to a central office of only thirty administrators. Having retained control of its affairs, the Catholic school maintained a sense of community even as the neighbourhood around it collapsed. The public school, neutered by administrative demands and paperwork, surrendered its sense of specialness to the social typhoons pounding on its doors. In so doing it became part of the typhoon.

Throughout North America it has become increasingly difficult to find schools, public or private, with a distinct mission or community culture. A few thrive on the margins of city life, where communities have resisted dismemberment by urbanization or the lust for owning things. Others have grown strong after disparate but determined citizens have joined forces to support good schooling as a common cause for their children. But these oases of learning are now the exception. In most North American towns, suburbs, and cities, the modern school has been severed from any real sense of community and from the very tradition of schooling itself. Schools, which once imparted local virtues, are now places where children learn to become strangers in a strange land.

This loss of community has been the work of educators and of several determined social forces. Over the last fifty years, as North American technocrats built bigger high schools and bigger school boards, parents slowly abandoned a system they could no longer understand and that could not, by dint of its size, remain true to the neighbourhood. Many parents, drawn by the demands of jobs far from home and bombarded by electronic media, retreated into suburban castles, trusting others to do what they no longer had time or the inclination even to think about. In this vacuum, educators naturally took over more and more of the duties normally expected of parents. The parent as participant in and proprietor of the educational system became the parent as client and captive.[2]

THE AGE OF EXPANSION

Like many North American institutions, the school system has become addicted to growth and all its trappings. As early as the 1950s, education had already become a major Canadian industry, costing $400 million a year or 1.8 per cent of the country's gross domestic product. By 1960 elementary and secondary schools had roughly doubled their required expenditures, to $1 billion or 3.2 per cent of the gross domestic product. In the 1980s the level of spending for these teaching centres (excluding universities and community colleges) reached $26 billion.

Although the end of the baby boom has slowed the growth of educational spending, Canadians still pay $32 billion for basic schooling a year and employ just under 300,000 teachers. (When one adds post-secondary education and another 63,500 teachers, the total cost soars to $52 billion.) Teachers now instruct — or, rather, "facilitate learning opportunities" — for 4.5 million students. *The Economist*, the British magazine, recently congratulated Canada for setting aside a higher proportion (7.2 per cent) of its GDP for education than any other industrial country "without being conspicuously successful." Japan, by contrast, spends 4.9 per cent of its GDP for schooling with conspicuously good results in the elementary grades. The United States spends 5.7 per cent of its GDP (or $300 billion) with dismal results right down the line.

The great and costly expansion of North American education was driven by the baby boom and glorified by two distinct advocates. One group, mainly economists, promoted the idea that schooling, "the cultivation of human resources," contributed in a big way to economic growth. They cited economic studies that announced a new and remarkable fact of life: "Between any two groups of individuals of the same age and sex, the one with more education will have higher average earnings than the one with less." Given the demands of science, technology, and consumerism, argued the economists, the industrial world needed more schools to produce higher wage earners capable of inventing more things to buy. The economists apparently perceived no limit to this consumptive craziness.

The other progressive proponents of expansion were liberal social activists who believed that schools were such powerful weapons against unemployment, drug abuse, poverty, racism, and illiteracy that North America needed more of them. The same kind of thinking that accompanied the nuclear build-up also led to its educational equivalent: the more we have, the brighter our future will be.

Both groups spoke with inflated rhetoric. The economists forgot about the principle of supply and demand. They also neglected to mention that if the schools really did their job, the economy would fall apart trying to employ all those willing and able minds. The social activists forgot that time spent on feel-good activities and social agendas was time subtracted from the demanding enterprise of learning. They also didn't understand that if one is concerned about establishing a more humane society, the most appropriate place to start is where people live and work.

These dangerous assumptions went unquestioned during the school boom because most governments could afford to throw money at the schools. Now, as funds dwindle and schools close, the failed rhetoric of the expansion years threatens to leave our most important public enterprise in perilous decline, without political friends or much community support.

One of the hidden aspects of the spending spree over the last three decades has been its lack of effectiveness. Since the 1960s, more than two hundred studies have examined the relationship between the amount of money being poured into schools and the performance of students. Most of these studies have failed to find any laudable connection. One Canadian study of school boards even found an inverse relationship. It seems that free-spending school districts in British Columbia, dubbed Moribund and Halfheart by the researchers, rarely achieved good student performance because they treated quality as a commodity that could be purchased. Thrifty boards, however, got good results because they concentrated on the essentials of teaching and learning.

These same studies also found that a classroom's major cost — the number of degrees attached to a teacher's name (the chief determinant of his or her income) — didn't seem to make much of a difference. Neither did class size. In fact, a steady drop in student-teacher ratios from 26-1 to about 18-1 in the last thirty years has not significantly bettered student achievement or narrowed the learning gap between working-class and middle-class students. It has, however, employed more educators. Margarete Wolfram, an educational pyschologist at York University, recently observed that the goal of the public school used to be to prepare the next generation.

"But now its only purpose seems to be to create employment for the present generation."

These findings on the illusory benefits of high spending do not mean that there are no important qualitative differences among teachers and schools. It's just that these differences rarely have anything to do with money. Throwing tax dollars at schools is not a guarantee of quality. The religion of spending, whether practised by families or school boards, has never been a substitute for hard work and moral purpose.

Another legacy of the spending boom has been the phenomenal growth of educational bureaucracies. Albert Shanker, the effusive president of the American Federation of Teachers (he also writes a weekly column for the *New York Times*), recently calculated that the state of New York employed more educational administrators than did all of western Europe. This explosion of bureaucrats is not restricted to that one state. In 1950 teachers represented 70 per cent of the educators in American schools; today they represent only 54 per cent.

Statistics on the multiplication of educrats in Canada are hard to come by, but Canadian school boards have unquestionably copied the American experience by hiring more technocrats to meet the escalating demands of special interest groups, legislators, teachers' unions, and regulatory agencies. In 1972 Newfoundland had twenty-four consultants, clinicians, and non-teaching personnel. Ten years later the number had swelled, astoundingly, to 381. In Manitoba the number jumped from 185 to 631, in Saskatchewan from 237 to 802, and so forth. During this ten-year period, meanwhile, school enrolment in these provinces was actually declining.[3]

In 1969 in Ontario, Canada's most populous province, one board looked after 19,000 students with a head office of twenty-two employees. In 1991 the number of students had more than doubled, to 42,000. Over those same two decades, the support staff had grown by a factor of 18, to four hundred. So, too, has the paperwork multiplied for principals and superintendents. (The Calgary Board of Education suffers similar imbalances: it employs 5,564 full-time teachers and 3,268 non-teaching staff!)

These bureaucracies have a curious way of eating money. Studies in the United States have shown that board office salaries consume $3,000 out of the $6,000 appropriated for every student. Of the $3,000 that actually reached the school, $1,000 got lost in head-office administrative costs. If that study is indicative, only about one-third of the money directly allocated for students ever reaches its intended destination.

In a 1990 study of modern schooling, two researchers from the Brookings Institution concluded that the growth of bureaucracy was fundamentally harming public education. "Many public school systems seem to have become so bureaucratized that their schools cannot possibly develop clear objectives and high academic expectations or attract and keep the kinds of principals and teachers that are required for effective performance."[4]

Just as the Canadian oil industry did during the boom of the 1970s, educators have spent, built, and added on programs and services without any coherent plan or realistic sense of limits. Unlike the oil patch today, however, educational institutions cannot be effectively regulated or reformed by market forces. As essentially social monopolies, they appear to have become unmanageable because of their autonomous nature. "They are closed-in motors which can now idle or run on full load and can only be shut down if their power supply is cut off," recently noted Norberto Bottani, a European school expert. Many of the ongoing battles between concerned parents and professional educators really boil down to this question: do we build smaller, controllable motors, or do we ration the fuel?

THE WATERMELON SCHOOL

To appreciate how the structure of the school has changed under the pressures of bureaucrats, unlimited growth, and uninvolved parents, think of the institution as a fruit and of its skin, flesh, and seeds as its three constituent parts. From time immemorial the adults (or seeds) have set the tone. The students (or flesh) have always mirrored the values of the community at large. The protective seal of elders (the skin) historically established constraints and policies.

At the turn of the century, Canadian and American schools looked more like healthy avocados. At the centre was a group of unified adults with a strong sense of doing something worthwhile. The meaty middle layer of students was fairly homogeneous and rural in character. The skin — the school's external policy, set largely by a stable community — was thin and well-defined.

By the 1950s, however, most schools had come to resemble cantaloupes. The fruit had grown in size to accommodate an expanded and more diverse middle-class body. The skin, too, had become thicker, thanks to examination systems, social goals, and a burgeoning new bureaucracy. But there was still plenty of room at the centre for teachers and principals to do the right thing.

Now, in the turbulent 1990s, North America's incoherent communities have sprouted schools that are more like overripe watermelons. The inch-thick rind represents three decades of bureaucracy, progressive rhetoric, brave new curricula, union contracts, and bibles of political correctness. The fruit is now an immensely diverse student body of poor and rich, black and white, straight and gay, English-speaking and non-English-speaking. In the midst of this great pluralistic mass, the centre of authority has disappeared. Like watermelon seeds, adult specialists float about here and there, issuing commands from a variety of locations, often at cross purposes.

Watermelon schools share three distinct characteristics. They are, first and foremost, the antithesis of a community. With their assistant principals, secretaries, social workers, pyschologists, language consultants, multicultural experts, full-time aides, and on-duty policemen, they symbolize not a community with common goals and values but rather a proliferation of competing professional cultures.

The watermelon is expected to be a universal receptor, to absorb more and more water without ever bursting. Because there is no central authority, each professional group willingly takes on more mandates and assignments. While parents park their children in day-care centres and mental institutions dump their charges in the streets, the schools are being told that they must house everyone and keep them happy, regardless of the consequences for teachers or students or the community itself.

In the watermelon school, any kind of behaviour is tolerated if it has not been declared illegal. In such a value-neutral environment, students have more rights than responsibilities; the faceless technocracy exercises no power beyond limp edict. In creating such "purposive disorder," believes Gerald Grant, a California researcher who came up with the watermelon analogy, North Americans have made expensive boxes where children "receive the administrations of a greatly enlarged core of specialists in a setting in which presumed equals argue about their rights, and individuals pursue their moral preferences in whatever direction they please, so long as they do not break the law."

The effects of these changes have been profound. A 1992 survey of four thousand Canadian teenagers born between 1973 and 1977 found that they wanted more things, more choices, and more rights than their parents. As offspring of the Me Generation and products of the watermelon school, they also placed much less value on honesty, generosity, intelligence, and politeness than adolescents did a decade ago. "People should practise safe sex, eat more veggies, and listen to lots of Led Zeppelin," said one fifteen-year-old male student. Added a Montreal high school student, in contrast, "It makes me sad to see the disintegration of traditional support networks — the family, community and religion. We need a sense of our roots. We need a past so we can create a future."[5]

The steady growth of these watermelon institutions has irrevocably changed the way educators define schools. When sprawling cities and advancing technologies all but destroyed smaller, community-minded schools — the avocado model — educators started to gauge school progress in purely technocratic and material terms. Suddenly good schools, as Tom Wolfe caustically observed, looked like "a duplicating machine replacement-parts wholesale distribution warehouse." Adopting the language of systems analysts and efficiency experts, educators spoke of "inputs": costlier buildings, faster buses, newer computers, more dirt-resistant rugs. They no longer measured quality by the intelligence and character of the young citizens they graduated but by the quantity of material goods or services they were able to provide for their pupils. If a school increased its library facilities, reduced teacher-pupil ratios, and added more non-teaching support staff, all was well in the watermelon patch.

It rarely dawns on the modern educator, as Dennis Cassivi notes in *Education and the Cult of Modernism*, to ask the most fundamental question: "What difference do elaborate buildings, nifty class schedules and computerized timetables make if the children are not learning?"

Conditioned by a culture dominated by the values of sales and marketing, the public also assumed that if lots of money was being spent on schools, only good things could happen. Joey Smallwood, the progressive premier of Newfoundland in the 1960s, embodied the North American optimism in the material approach to education: "Eighty-four schools with indoor toilets — that was Newfoundland on the day that I became premier. Today: 838 schools have indoor toilets. We have not in those years produced any new or original educational theory, philosophy or practices. But we have put indoor toilets in 744 schools that didn't have them. That's progress." Despite this educational progress, Newfoundland's students still score among the lowest on the continent in international math, science, and geography tests.

THE ILLICH EFFECT

In the 1970s the great Viennese philosopher Ivan Illich observed that the growth of modern schooling contained two important paradoxes. He found that the more money North Americans spend on schools, the more they discouraged other institutions from being involved in teaching and learning. The expansion of North America's educational institutions has been accompanied by a growing dependency on the institution among parents and businessmen. The "Illich effect" partly explains why neither Canada nor the United States has good apprenticeship programs, why so many parents have essentially given up on parenting, and why most corporations — from newspapers to mining companies — treat in-service training as cavalierly as they treat the cleaning staff. In a strange way, the unrestricted growth of the schools in North America has not only destroyed the public's romance with schooling but diminished public respect for learning in general.

The second paradox Illich found was that the more monopolistic the school, the more it ignored what people value most: the learning of skills and new ideas. Instead of upholding what schools of old did well — basic training in reading, writing, and languages — the new monolithic school made "this kind of drill teaching rare and disreputable." In place of the public agenda, educators now substitute what they themselves want to see accomplished: therapy and day care. The modern bureaucratic school almost precludes the learning of skills, Illich believes, and it has done an even worse job of providing what used to be called "an education."

The people largely responsible for the mess we've made of public education make up a new secular class, people the social critic Wendell Berry calls "itinerant professional vandals." The first characteristic of these education technocrats is that they have no allegiance to place and no local view. The modern educator, unlike his or her traditional counterpart, tends not to think of the classroom or school as a home but rather as a stepping stone on a career path. By definition, upwardly mobile professional transients cannot permit a school posting to interrupt their personal advance. Modern educators routinely jeopardize children, ignore program research, and circumvent concerned parents to ensure the success of their own careers or to promulgate their own feel-good theories about schooling. As Wendell Berry put it, "In order to be able to desecrate, endanger or destroy a place, after all, one must be able to leave it and to forget it."

The second characteristic of modern administrators is that they have seemingly floated from television cradles into elementary school, high school, university, faculty of education, and back into the school without any worldly interruptions. The minds of this group, unpolluted by community discourse and often devoid of intellectual substance or even curiosity, have been shaped by other educators. What matters to these people, first and foremost, are their professional commitments and personal ambitions. Given their priorities, it is perhaps not surprising that many educators no longer even believe in the value of literacy. Many are illiterate themselves.[6]

These professional functionaries usually come equipped with degrees in social work, physical education, psychology, or "education." Achieving their positions without ever having studied or loved a subject — literature, say, or science — modern administrators are disinclined to value someone who does. As a consequence, they assign music teachers to special education, math teachers to history, and phys ed instructors to calculus. Such everyday decisions, based on the demands of schedules and budgets, not only diminish the teachers involved but abuse the students. And so we find the itinerant professional vandals logically saluting the business of "education" while subverting the enterprise of learning.

Every secular class comes with its own set of beliefs, and modern educators are no exception. A recent Ontario study by Mark Holmes, a no-nonsense educator, of the attitudes and beliefs of chief education officers found what parents who care about children have long suspected: very few of these technocrats reflect the pluralistic communities they represent. Most are middle-aged white men who don't believe in capital punishment and attend the United Church. There is not much colour in this crowd, and very few Baptists, Buddhists, or Marxists. Not surprisingly, the élites who run school boards tend to vote Liberal in Canada (and Democrat in the United States).

These CEOs tend to describe their work as demanding, exciting, and political — but not pedagogical. In fact, most spend only 20 per cent of their time delivering and assessing school curricula and personnel. This inattentiveness to what was once the very foundation of public education accurately reflects the CEOs' commitment to providing children with individualized feel-good opportunities. Of six historic school models, the CEOs typically rank child-centred education as their first or second choice. Other philosophies of education — preparing pupils for work (technocratic), developing their intellectual and artistic lives (cultural), or shaping their characters (traditional) — just don't appeal to this bunch.

In contrast to the nation's educational bosses, ordinary citizens usually selected the cultural or the technocratic philosophy as their first choice. The progressive school ranked fifth in public favour; the prevailing folk wisdom was that schools should cultivate intellectual and social skills as well as prepare students for good citizenship and livelihood in a democracy. To the public, providing value-free fun and games has never seemed the appropriate mandate of education.

This discrepancy also shows up in attitudes towards testing and curriculum. A 1985 Gallup Poll showed that 94 per cent of the public considered regular and standardized assessments of student achievement important; only 15 per cent of educators considered such assessments important. Ninety-four per cent of the people polled identified a common national curriculum as important; only 20 per cent of the educators agreed with the people. Clearly, a Great Educational Divide has arisen between school bosses and the people they ostensibly serve.

WHO'S IN CHARGE HERE?

The degree to which schools have become inflexible and autonomous institutions ultimately serving a secular class of professionals became clear to Evelyn Dodds in 1985. That's the year she became a school trustee of the Lakehead Board of Education in northwestern Ontario and a populist champion of standards and quality. At the time, the former elementary school teacher and mother of three still harboured the illusion that public schools were answerable to the public.

Now, after years of fighting, she knows better. Canadians no longer have a public school system, she has concluded, but rather a "state-imposed empire" in which the employees, not the taxpayers, control standards, set rules, and spend money. Her attempts to question this monopoly have been painful and costly. Hostile school administrators have publicly attacked her as a latter-day "Hitler" and a "barracuda." Angry teachers in the Lakehead have picketed the board office, vandals have slashed her car tires, and BB pellets have been fired through the front window of her house. Along the way, Dodds developed stomach ulcers.

The battle reached fever pitch in 1988, when a slate of reform-minded trustees known as the Action Team elected Dodds chairman of the board. Her modest agenda included clear goals, standardized tests, the use of textbooks, and fiscal reform. Like most North American boards, the Lakehead Board of Education — with 17,000 pupils, 1,200 teachers, 1,100 bureaucrats, and 50 schools — had a no-limits-to-growth history. Although it had closed twenty schools in two decades, its budget rose from $80 million in 1985 to $130 million in 1990. Dodds wondered whether — in light of this burgeoning expenditure — local citizens were getting value for their money or good performance from the students.

The first sign of administrative intransigence appeared after Dodds and her reformers passed a resolution calling for "sequential ordered goals of knowledge" in spelling and grammar for the elementary grades. Dodds didn't want anything fancy, just measurable items for each grade, such as the mastery of active verbs or the correct spelling of two-syllable words.

The Lakehead's progressive administrators refused to comply, saying that they had to maintain ministry guidelines, which directed that they "must provide pupils with a secure, stimulating environment that will support and encourage the growth of self-confident, creative individuals." Grammar and spelling weren't part of the mandate. The administrators pointed out that the Lakehead Board of Education didn't teach such subjects separately, but rather folded them into a much grander smorgasbord called Language Arts. Trust our $100,000-a-year, taxpayer-funded experts, the bureaucrats effectively said to Dodds.

Ten months later, these educational experts published a jargon-laden document laying out the board's goals. These so-called goals included "appreciation of stories," "enjoying creative writing," and "awareness of commas." Students didn't have to demonstrate any mastery of skills, just a lot of appreciation. "That battle took two years," Dodds recalls, "and there are still no knowledge-based goals for English spelling and grammar."

Dodds next tried a resolution calling on teachers to correct student notebooks daily, since kids were coming home with unchecked work peppered with mistakes. There's plenty of educational research to show that a daily corrections routine tells teachers how well they have taught, and students how much they have learned. Principals and superintendents in the Lakehead gave the notion a thumbs down. "They said a committee of professionals had reviewed the resolution," Dodds says, "and said it was contrary to Ontario's educational philosophy."

Instead of implementing the trustees' (and, by extension, the local community's) will, the board's bureaucrats merely added an innocuous clause to an already innocuous policy on evaluation. Correcting mistakes, of course, is not the same as evaluating a student's work.

"It was sheer insubordination," says Dodds. "They didn't develop the policy we wanted."

The battle heated up. When Dodds asked for dictionaries for elementary school children, half the board's teachers refused to participate in a simple book inventory. When Dodds set aside money for "relevant teaching materials such as textbooks," administrators bought more films and sandboxes.

Occasionally, Dodds scored a victory. It took four years of vicious wrangling, but Thunder Bay students now write standardized tests in Grades 6 and 9, and trustees get a report card on the results. When one principal told Dodds that she had no right to ask for that kind of information, she replied testily, "I see. I'm just supposed to pay you and go home."

Evelyn Dodds is just one example of the divorce between parents and educators. More broadly, this rift is evident in the exclusive language and professional jargon with which school administrators hide or justify their deeds. Like all such jargon, it salutes the future and provides the illusion that educators are efficient prognosticators. A 1972 Alberta report on educational planning (*A Choice of Futures*), for example, begins: "We are not merely parts of the future; taken together we are its cause....This report represents a choice of futures in the same way that a television schedule represents a choice of features." By selling faith in the future, educators enable themselves to impose any innovation or silliness on the grounds that they are preparing children for "participation in a changing world."

Educators also have a knack of stringing words together in long phrases that convey little thought or meaning — "confluent educational strategies and interactive processes of communication between the child, the teacher and the world," and so forth. They seem to live by the Piet Hein maxim: "If your thoughts are rubbish merely, don't express yourself too clearly." The impoverished writing of these bureaucrats also reflects their prejudice that writing is a personal means of communication rather than a public commitment to clarity.[7]

As the Canadian prairie activist Hilda Neatby observed years ago, educational jargon, unlike scientific or legal gobbledygook, has the air of a priestly caste. Its purpose — whether educators happen to be pontificating on "Sociocognitive Correlates of Prejudice in Children," "Expectations Raised by Androgyny," or "The Power of Didactic Interaction as Cross-cultural Communications" — is to mystify ideas and thereby guard them from outside examination. Such language glorifies process, stifles criticism, and builds status among other educators. In such an environment, even simple ideas (rudeness) become inflated notions (disinviting behaviour).

Like most academics, educators are not deeply concerned about communicating with the commons. The consequences of this retreat into incomprehension are obvious to everyone except educators: ideas about schooling and its outcomes flow less freely or not at all; meanwhile, the public's trust in educators sinks to ever-lower depths because goals are never expressed in language that is plain or manageable.

This inability to communicate clearly with ordinary people is perhaps most telling in the modern use of the word "education." In its fullest sense, "to educate" means to bring up young people in the culture and traditions of their parents so that they're better able to serve their community. But the modern educator has supplanted this definition with two technocratic meanings: one refers to the techniques and statistical knowledge used to manage schools; the other refers to the mass of academic theory that flows like lava out of the continent's faculties of education. When educators talk about "education" these days, they're usually talking about ways of extending their control over public life.

DIMINISHED FACULTIES

At the root of much of this technocratic arrogance are the nation's faculties of education. Here beginning teachers and novice administrators receive a thorough indoctrination. Ask teachers about the quality of this training and most will spout a litany of woes. They'll document Mickey Mouse courses, worthless theories, ignorant professors (some of whom have not been in a classroom for twenty years), and a grinding anti-intellectualism. In fact, most will state that their training had nothing to do with effective teaching.

The average teacher now enters the classroom clutching a four-year bachelor of education degree, which includes a three-year liberal arts degree, about 1,600 hours of professional study (that's one year's worth), and ten weeks of practice teaching. Excluding the liberal arts degree, that's little more than the formal training given a barber, meat cutter, or assistant cook. Like barber schools, faculties of education aren't known for their academic rigour. It may be difficult to gain access to one; once inside, however, participants find it easy to get out with A's. This grade inflation does not mean the modern teacher is a literate citizen. On the contrary, many would-be teachers enrolled in faculties of education have difficulty spelling simple English words or even composing a sentence.[8]

Perhaps a profession dominated by religious enthusiasm for "discovery" and "activity" can't help but hail the obscure and shun the exact. Many teachers graduate from faculties of education without ever having taken a course on curriculum design (long-term planning), evaluation and measurement ("Was my teaching effective?"), reading ("What methods work with whom?"), or special education ("How do you teach the hard-to-teach?"). That's tantamount to letting medical students skip nutrition, diagnosis, and pediatrics.

Student teachers get a smorgasbord of courses such as "Developing a Personal Philosophy of Education" — a class that lets people with no teaching experience suddenly create an individual philosophy, and involves lots of discussion and the keeping of a personal narrative. This kind of incoherent and disjointed training once prompted the behavioural pyschologist, B.F. Skinner, to observe that "teaching is the only respectable profession that has no instructional training."

This also explains why teacher trainers systematically ignore the principles of good teaching. When supervising student teachers, they grade lesson preparations or flashy routines, rather than assessing whether the children learned anything from the teaching. This emphasis on presentation styles has unfortunate consequences. Student teachers learn that there is one good presentation style: the one professors grade with an A. Trainees who get A's think they've developed excellent teaching habits, virtually guaranteeing a lifetime of teaching children or managing a school with no self-criticism. Studies on teacher decision making show that, once teachers get a plan in their head, they're often not flexible enough to change it, even if it's obvious that what they're doing is not working well.

A brief from the British Columbia Principals and Vice Principals Association to the British Columbia College of Teachers found that teacher education may look good on paper but fails in implementation because the faculties "are isolated from the real classroom, resistant to input from the field and unresponsive to the demands of public policy." It concluded that many faculty members "are poor models of good teaching and lack recent classroom experience."

BABBLE AND THEORY

What is education, as professional educators live it? Let's visit, with a Nova Scotia elementary school teacher, a masters of education program at the Ontario Institute for Studies in Education (OISE) in Toronto. At the institute, teachers routinely take courses in order to move their provincial salary scales up a notch. This particular teacher took half a dozen courses in the "Curriculum" department, where professors made the assumption that one could design a course without any thought about subject matter. Although two courses on linguistics and European education were well-taught, the rest showed little respect for teaching, learning, or public money. "Nothing OISE offered (except the course on linguistics) did anything to make me a better, or more knowledgeable classroom teacher," says the graduate.

In a letter to the institute, the teacher documented how instructors cancelled classes unexpectedly or wasted much time with idle chitchat, late starts, and early finishes. These well-paid academics, all devotees of child-centred education, expected their adult students to take part in childish activities. Some required prospective teachers to walk around in circles reading poetry; others opened the class by pantomiming instructions and passing around potato chips. A few administered psychological tests without explaining their purpose (personal research) or securing individual permission. The work load was lighter than that of a university undergraduate program; in no course did the reading assignments average a book a week. Not surprisingly, the courses were poorly designed. Course readings and course content were rarely connected. A class on children's literature lacked a syllabus; halfway through it, the professor asked: "Where should we go from here?"

Most instructors also seemed oblivious to the relationship between marking and learning. Daily assignments in one course were due the last day of class, violating the basic principle that improvement requires regular feedback. Essays received comments so vague — "Interesting approach and analysis" — as to suggest that they hadn't been read. The Nova Scotia teacher learned that it was easier to get an A at OISE than in her own Grade 6 classroom. She also found that many of her fellow colleagues, all native Canadians, couldn't speak, spell, or write their native language with any mastery. These future teachers wrote of "deterents" and "adgendas" and constructed sentences that would dismay Strunk and White: "Often, especially in books for children, a collection of myths are presented."

The instructors displayed similar symptoms of inadequate literacy. One academic, in a draft paper for an Ontario history consultant's seminar, wrote: "Surely, it is the most unsatisfactory type of planning that lead to the publication of a recent OHASSTA resolution that read 'that there be a compulsory course in Modern World History at the Grade 11-12 level.' This statement, by itself, which is how it is stated, is difficult to accept."

The teacher from Nova Scotia was further dismayed by the anti-intellectualism of the OISE staff. Professors suggested leisure studies should have priority over Shakespeare because students, after all, must be prepared for the future. One facilitator even chastised the Nova Scotian "for being shocked that a Grade I teacher of my acquaintance didn't know how many syllables the word 'bridge' had."

Such testimonies are common, and they explain why so many teachers know nothing about fair evaluations, sequential teaching, or meaningful report cards. Parents know that they cannot expect their child to value or practise what they themselves ridicule and debase every day. Yet this is exactly what teacher training demands of teachers.

Many university professors secretly regard faculties of education as regrettable and disdainful places, yet these faculties are representative of university education these days. They symbolize how little universities actually value what was once at the heart of education: teaching and learning.

North America's teacher-training system now creates educational technicians with limited life experience who are more interested in social work, therapy, or political transformation than in teaching a subject well. After being immersed in a culture of babble and theory, small wonder so many educators can no longer identify a pedagogical problem, let alone fix it. Nor is it any wonder that so many parents no longer trust educators. In some ways, the goals of these two groups have become inimical. Most educators are primarily concerned about the survival of their empire. Most parents still want what parents have always wanted: a good education for their children.

The abysmal quality of training in education faculties mirrors the farcical quality of much educational research. Never has so much been written about so little for such incestuous readers.

"Educational researchers," observes Dennis Cassivi, himself an educational researcher, "are that breed of mankind who have made a career out of pursing senseless questions with a vigor and technical precision that makes the exercise both bizarre and extravagant." They typically ask only what can be answered easily: "How many people in Halifax like universities and to what extent?" "Do teachers in Chicago use overhead projectors in their classrooms and how often and under what circumstances?"

Cassivi's own contribution to the publishing circus was a 284-page dissertation that asked teachers what they thought about teacher training in Nova Scotia. The short answer was "bloody awful." Yet, writes Cassivi, he tried to convince himself that he was researching something important and making a contribution even though every teacher knew the answer. "This is the stuff of which careers are made."

Educators' academic celebration of the trivial, the stupid, and the anecdotal — all in unreadable prose — partly explains why few teachers read educational research or trust its conclusions. Fewer than a quarter of elementary teachers ever read professional journals. Most are much more likely to pick up *TV Guide* than *Educational Leadership*.

This distrust of research also explains why educators are ignorant of the perhaps 5 per cent of the literature that actually addresses real instructional issues. Ask most administrators about the studies on effective schools, direct instruction, or the importance of systematic phonics teaching for beginning readers, and their faces will go blank as foolscap. But ask them about "planetary awareness" or the joys of self-esteem and they'll pour forth the lastest pyscho-babble.[9]

Educators frequently show the poverty of their technocratic indoctrination by their fickle love affairs with new techniques and dazzling innovations. Like adolescents who hate parent rule on principle, the modern educator generally dislikes and discards whatever has come before him. This keenness to obliterate the past makes the technocrats running our schools vulnerable to the endless succession of popular fads that move like waves through North America's classrooms.

These fads — such things as New Math, the Open Classroom, Whole Language, Invented Spelling, Talking Typewriters, Self-Esteem, and Global Education — all have three things in common. They were implemented in ostentatious haste without being properly tested in a variety of classrooms; they blamed any failure on the child; and they were usually advocated by administrators who had little understanding of the realities of teaching.

Consider New Math (which is now the old math). It was hastily composed by a group of scholars at MIT after the Soviet Union put a man in space ahead of the Americans. Fearing the low quality of North American math instruction had something to do with this Soviet success, educators demanded new programs. The result was a game-like curriculum that taught "Commutativity and Associativity" with the goal of promoting insight and comprehension rather than meaningless manipulation and recitation.

A slight problem arose after New Math had become a classroom staple: many of its graduates couldn't add, subtract, multiply, or divide. New Math is now gone (the current and equally ineffective trend is Discovery Math)[10] and with it the program's best idea: that learners ought to know the why of what they are being asked to compute.

The Open Classroom suffered similar shortcomings. Developed as a "style of teaching involving flexiblity of space, student choice of activity, richness of learning materials, integration of curriculum areas and more individual or small group than large group instruction,"[11] it entered North American schools with no research base. Nevertheless, technocrats tore down the walls and put sixty students, organized in four pods, all in the same room. They rationalized such openness by suggesting that it would make children more creative and better human beings. In the end nothing got taught. Nobody paid attention. In the noisy and Darwinian environment of the open classroom, the academically poor merely got poorer while the academically rich — especially those who could shut out the noise and read — got marginally richer. Ten years after its introduction, more than two hundred studies concluded that its lack of effectiveness did not "inspire much confidence" in the approach. Yet the trend has reappeared in recent years with a new name: "program continuity" and "multi-aged classrooms."

THE COMPUTER PANACEA

One of the latest classroom fashions sweeping North American schools is computers. School administrators intent on relevance now talk and breathe computers the way they praised the open classroom two decades ago. True to technocratic tradition, most school administrators have asked few questions and read little research about the true value of computer-assisted learning. As a consequence, they have spent millions of other people's dollars on largely bogus products.

The history of this latest boondoggle is short but grim. In the late 1970s, educators and businessmen began championing the computer as a revolutionary cure-all that would create higher-achieving students, more dynamic schools, and a competitive work-force for the Information Age. Some propagandists suggested that the computer would replace teachers altogether. Most just mouthed the powerful but misleading notion that the quality of education would magically rise in direct proportion to the number of computers purchased.[12]

Nearly every elementary classroom in North America now has at least one computer. Most Canadian high schools have somewhere between twenty-five and fifty machines. Some experimental schools, such as Vancouver's Virtual High, have gone totally high-tech, with a machine for each pupil. But all these computers have not only failed to deliver any of the promised goods, they have exacerbated many old school inequalities. Crippled by a lack of solid research, clear guidance, and useful software, the majority of the $2,000 IBMs and Macs in our schools now function as expensive flash cards, glitzy typewriters, or New Age furniture.

Like many educational innovations, the computer blitz puts the cart before the horse. Computers can't make a difference in the classroom without good programs. By and large, existing programs are really nothing more than books with chapter headings. Unless a teacher does the time-consuming and creative work of making the program useful, then nothing appears on the screen that's not available in a book.

Contrary to the predictions that computers would replace bad teachers or mitigate the consequences of their poor teaching, the opposite has occurred. Given the time and work it takes to turn computers into useful tools, only the most skilled and able instructors have dared integrate the machine into their classrooms. Even in these cases, 90 per cent of all software packages end up gathering dust on shelves within four months of being purchased.[13]

Whenever teachers have tried to enhance writing, reading, or problem-solving skills with computers, the results have not been promising. In math, computers do seem to increase student achievement, but as a supplement to rather than a substitute for regular instruction. Using a computer absolutely improves a student's attitude to computers, but it doesn't seem to have any positive effect on his or her attitude towards the subject being taught. In short, computers do a poor job of sustaining interest in matters of educational importance.

Administrators tend not to read the research that would tell them all this. Nor do they ever ask teachers, "How much more are we asking you to do?" or "Where is the time and training to come from?" Most North American teachers have received fewer than ten hours of computer training. As they did with the open classroom and New Math, technocrats paid more attention to the flash and glitter of the tool than to training the tool users.

Many teachers know how grossly their administrators have wasted public funds but are reluctant to say so publicly for obvious reasons. One Ottawa history teacher recently explained the misspent-funds phenomenon this way: "Who among us has not, at one time or another, watched and subsequently succumbed to a demonstration of some wonderful gadget by purchasing it — vegetable choppers spring to mind — only to find it either impossible to reproduce the demonstrated results at home or to find out it demanded so much time and effort to do so that it was faster and easier to complete the job in some other way." In spite of the computer's shortcomings, administrators press on, setting weekly computer quotas for students and even monitoring teacher compliance. In doing so, the educators set up teachers as the scapegoats for their own administrative follies.

To compound this financial and pedagogical irresponsibility, teachers acknowledge the computer fad to be a costly folly in one breath, but then lip sync the administrative justification for pushing ahead anyway. "We must ensure," so the argument goes, "the development of better equipment and software for our use tomorrow, by providing today the incentive of a healthy market to the producers of these goods." The same history teacher, threatened with dismissal if he spoke publicly about computer fraud in his school board, doesn't know anyone who would use the same approach when spending his or her own money. "Can you imagine a person saying he'll buy a particular car today that doesn't really meet his needs, because he wants to encourage car manufacturers to build better cars that he can then buy in the future?"

A NEW KIND OF IDIOCY

Progressive educators have created schools that make the child's "personality development" their guiding principle. To question the wisdom of allowing children to direct their own curriculum or moral development under the watchful eye of facilitators is to question goodness and happiness itself. As Jacques Ellul notes in *The Technological Society*, the new psychopedagogical technique comes with three totalitarian features. First, it holds that only the state is capable of raising "self-adjusted" or "self-realized" individuals, which effectively means "the end of private instruction and therefore of a traditional freedom." (Consider, for example, the educators' almost uniform interpretation of home schooling as an attack on public schooling.) Second, it insists that it be rigorously extended to all children (hence the little choice provided in public schools). And third, it applies itself aggressively to the ideal that the child must somehow be freed from the confines of family and community.

This new freedom, of course, entails a daily manipulation of the child's thoughts and feelings, as well as a reshaping of his spiritual life, preparation for entry into what educators call "a fluid regenerating society."

Instead of the liberation of the child, progressives are really achieving a new kind of social conformity. Despite all the preposterous talk about catering to the child's feelings and interests, the goal of the modern school is really to pleasantly indoctrinate him or her to accept and live in a brave new world. The progressive typically believes that he is fighting a historic battle against "standardization, superficiality and commercialism of industrial society." In fact, he is really just aiding in the production of a new kind of conforming idiocy.[14]

Ellul and most critics of the progressive agenda have no doubt that modern schooling achieves what it promises: seemingly happier and better-balanced people. But this, he argues, is precisely its danger: "It makes men happy in a milieu which normally would have made them unhappy, if they had not been worked on, molded, and formed for just that milieu. What looks like the apex of humanism is in fact the pinnacle of human submission: children are educated to become precisely what society expects of them.

They must have social consciences that allow them to strive for the same ends as society sets for itself.... Any form of government or social transformation becomes possible with individuals who have experienced this never-ending process of adaptation. The key word of the new human techniques is, therefore, adaptation."

When educators say they are educating children "to embrace change with confidence" or "to work in a world characterized by justice, peace and the well-being of all," they are really saying that education has only one goal: to create value-free technicians and apprentices to whatever gimmick or gadget is useful. What was once an institution with a definite and limited function has become a chameleon that daily insinuates itself into the troubled domains of family and community. Having lost its communal character and populist perspective, the school has become most adept at the production of consumers, technicians, and more educators.

ALL OF THE ABOVE

The great divorce between educators and community is often highlighted by a newly popular educational gimmick, the questionnaire. Rather than calling a public meeting, where ideas can be debated openly and passionately, administrators send out ever-reliable multiple choice forms. Like politicians seeking to evade real scrutiny, educators admire questionnaires because they create the illusion of involvement. When Joseph Freedman, a Red Deer radiologist and father of two girls, received a thirty-three-question survey from his local board (Are you satisfied with the field trips at your son/daughter's school?), he replied with an angry letter that launched his career as one of Canada's best-informed school reformers. An angry Freedman wrote, "Your survey is ill-conceived. You have set the agenda, not the parent-user who pays for the system. To remind you, I am the user, not my child."

The results of these questionnaires are often incompletely reported. When the London (Ontario) Council of Home and School Associations surveyed two thousand parents in 1991, it concluded that citizens were "clearly concerned about the quality of their child's education; and about the education system generally." What was needed, suggested the report, was the predictable: more and better communication.

These facile summaries ignored some rather damning findings. Nearly a quarter of the parents reported going outside the system for tutorial help and only half expressed "satisfaction" with teaching in reading skills. Almost half the respondents registered "dissatisfaction" with teaching in spelling and grammar.

When a local parent reviewed 1,265 written commentaries that had accompanied the completed questionnaire, he found even greater evidence of unrest.[15] Only 8 per cent of the letters approved of the current state of affairs; 76 per cent voiced strong disapproval of the board's educational leadership. Although some of the parental commentary gave good reviews to teachers, not a single respondent "had a kind word for senior administrative staff." Parents uniformly viewed the powers-that-be as autocratic, unhelpful, and fiscally irresponsible.

One angry citizen wrote, "Generally the teachers fight a battle against stupidity, mediocrity, officiousness and self-centredness among administrators to whom they are obliged to report." A teacher added, "We have an abysmal language arts/reading program, no science or history, no geography, a math program that has almost reached the depths of the language program, but our lucky students get to spend a month studying 'pigs' in Grade 1. (Yes, folks, we are preparing them all for the service industry — or pig farming.)" Another taxpayer concluded, "Senior staff are definitely not accountable and our tax dollars are being wasted on 'perks' such as conferences in Niagara-on-the-Lake and 'retreats' for attendance counsellors at Oakwood Golf and Country Club."

The parent wisely concluded that more communication would not solve the problem. "Parents," he wrote, "know very well what is going on in the schools; they don't like it, and they believe that the education bureaucracy does not care whether they like it or not."

The dismissive and purposeless style of modern educators also extends to classroom veterans. Montana's Office of Public Instruction recently asked its teachers for "input" on reading programs "which will enable our students to step into the twenty-first century." The questionnaire asked teachers to describe their philosophy of reading, their recommendations for an ideal program based on the latest research, and the kind of assistance they wanted from technocrats at OPI.

Siegfried Engelmann, an outspoken Oregon researcher, wrote an understated response to the inquiry. It went like this: "You should be concerned with people who can answer your questions, because they know how to do it. To treat the game as a microcosm of democracy, or a consensus game, will yield more of what you already have, suggestions based on no knowledge of effective solutions. There are tons of studies that show how naive the general teacher, the average supervisor, and the typical principal are about instructional materials, diagnosis, and remedies. Your goal should be to upgrade these folks, not to solicit their advice. Shame on you."

These psychological games accentuate the totalitarian nature of much progressive dogma. Its special brand of relativism has never been tested by the will of communities that make up the public school system. It slipped like a thief into the school, with no vote and little discussion. Yet if the central tenets of John Dewey's philosophy had been submitted to a philosophical ballot, ordinary working people would have flatly rejected its dangerous conceits. For Dewey's central beliefs, then as now, conflict with what the commons hold most true: real learning, thrift, self-denial, and competence. Asked to fund and support schools where a child-centred dogma flouts eternal truths and fixed moral laws, the public would say no. Having been denied this right by professional educators, the public has predictably adopted hostile views about educators and schooling.

The widespread use of questionnaires in our school system demonstrates how educators conceive of their roles. Many believe they are delivering a product, whether it be self-realization or self-esteem, to a specialized market, a body of consumers known as students. The quality of the product and its delivery can be gauged only by its popularity, by how good it makes the students feel. (Many universities now rate instructors not on the basis of what their students have learned but on their standing in student opinion polls.)[16]

Because many educators know little of the history of public schooling, they don't realize that viewing education as a consumer product defeats the historic notion of schooling as a community enterprise. Unwittingly, they have forsaken their duty to uphold a public virtue that has always sought to evaluate its participants not on the basis of feelings, but on the quality of individual performance measured against standards of excellence.

CHAPTER FOUR

What's To Be Done?

"We must learn to live happily with less than we can dream of."   GARRETT HARDIN

THE ERODED PASTURE

North America's school system has become a "tragedy of the commons." Parents, teachers, and bureaucrats have behaved much like fifty families who own a community pasture. In the beginning, the pasture had a well-defined public focus: the equal feeding of fifty cows. When each member of the community placed only one cow on the common, all was well.

But as each member of the community sought to increase his own wealth and power by adding more cows to the pasture, the common fell from grace. In attempting to better their individual circumstances, the members forgot or ignored what the pasture could sustain. The additional cows multiplied and munched ever-dwindling patches of grass to their roots. The land eroded and became less productive.

The equivalent in the public school system of placing more cows on limited land has been the dumping of an endless array of missions, services, and curriculums on a community institution with finite resources. This purposeful over-grazing accounts for the aimlessness of the modern school and helps explain its virtual collapse.

The American biologist Garrett Hardin observed that freedom in a commons can bring ruin to all when participants in any public enterprise — hospitals, parks, schools — feel locked into a system that encourages people to increase their demands without limit in a world that is limited. In the tragedy of public education, all the participants share responsibility and, by implication, share an equally dismal future.

When any pasture becomes dangerously eroded, the owners have two options: slowly rebuild the land, or abandon it altogether. The slow and steady growth of private and religious schools over the past two decades in the United States (where they have attracted 12 per cent of all students), Canada (8 per cent), and Australia (25 per cent) shows that an increasing number of parents have chosen the latter option. Many have done so in the best interests of their children; they simply did not know how to rebuild a public property so thoroughly abused.

The retreat to private schools is, at best, a desperate and short-term solution. The private system is but a smaller fenced pasture that runs parallel to the public one. Every range manager knows that weeds thriving on poor, grazed-out land soon invade the surrounding land. The destruction of the public system weakens the ecology of its private neighbour by eroding borders and fouling joint water supplies. This helps explain why a strong public system can feed and sustain a strong private component, and why a weak public system ultimately diminishes private schools along with it.

When Ontario's public school system banished grammar instruction in high school (it remains as an option), the private system followed suit. Jone Schoeffel, a teacher at Havergal, an élite Toronto girls' school, who dared teach the logic of nouns and verbs during lunch time, was fired for being a "disturbing influence."

The reasons for these powerful connections and consequences between public and private schools are simple. Citizens who assume that private schools are inherently better than public ones forget that most private schools use the same untested and error-ridden textbooks, the same incoherent curricula, and the same floating standards as public schools. More important, both institutions recruit administrators infused with the same enthusiasms that sweep education as inevitably as new strains of influenza or new styles in the fashion industry. Private schools also employ teachers from the same abysmal factories of teacher indoctrination: faculties of education.[1]

Though the moral climate of many private schools is indeed superior to the moral chaos of their public cousins, the quality of instruction does not vary as much as many parents like to believe. Parents who send their children to private school, then, may be buying peace of mind but not necessarily good teaching.

DEFINING EXCELLENCE

Across North America a small minority of schools, both private and public, have escaped the tragedy of the commons. Some schools — certainly no more than 10 per cent — do function as effective community enterprises with a unity of purpose. How do they achieve this feat in the face of institutional discouragement? By prizing and developing six important characteristics. Taken together, these key features recognize the limits of schooling, give a school community purpose, and respect what actually works in the classroom. Research in England, the United States, and Canada has repeatedly identified the characteristics of effective schools for nearly twenty years. And for the same period, North American educators have practically ignored them. "We can, whenever and wherever we choose, successfully teach all children whose schooling is of interest to us," wrote the late Ronald Edmonds, an early American pioneer of effective schools research. "We already know more than we need, in order to do this. Where we do it must finally depend on how we feel about the fact we haven't so far."

The characteristics of a good school are easy to identify but difficult to create. They cannot be decreed from on high or sold as some kind of educational ready-mix. Good schools make themselves, one by one, and then stand alone, in spite of bad neighbourhoods, thoughtless educational policies, indifferent parents, and inept administrators. They hum with an energetic purpose and a moral vision. They offer their students a special counter-culture to the image-rich but spirit-poor consumerism outside their doors. Here's what good schools have in common.

1. Focus

Not surprisingly, every good school focuses on teaching and learning first. Effective elementary schools concentrate on the mastery of reading, writing, and math; effective high schools provide good teaching in a dozen basic subjects, on the grounds that less subject choice guarantees deeper knowledge and, ultimately, greater work choice. Father Grant, the former principal of St. Augustine High School, an excellent black school in Louisiana, summed up his mind-centred priorities this way: "Don't consume my time with extraneous issues and then expect me to have enough time left over to dedicate myself to a strong academic program where I will turn out strong, intelligent, competent kids."

The corollary is that effective schools don't boast a lot of frills. Their students usually spend four times the number of hours doing academic work than most public schools (where academic work is now estimated to occupy less than 20 per cent of the school day). Although the teaching methods in effective schools may vary from traditional to progressive, the schools all establish academic programs that get good results for all children and abandon programs that don't. Mark Holmes, a professor studying school effectiveness at the Ontario Institute for Studies in Education in Toronto, notes: "The evidence overwhelmingly shows that the degreee to which the school aggressively works towards academic goals is related to its success in achieving those goals." This doesn't mean that good schools are technocratic, boring, or authoritarian. On the contrary, they understand that regular physical exercise, music, art, and laughter all contribute to their climates of high achievement.

2. Homework

Good schools provide regular and meaningful homework. Aside from reinforcing learning and building good study habits, homework demands a unifying collaboration among teacher, parent, and child. It reminds all three parties that they are involved in a common endeavour.

In a 1980 study of 1,015 Catholic, public, and non-religious private schools, the American sociologist James Coleman found that regular homework assignments partly explained why students at private and Catholic schools outperformed public school students by a full academic year. In nightly assignments, which built on what had been taught during the day and were promptly corrected, Catholic and private students did a total of 4.92 hours of homework per week — at least one hour more than their public peers.

3. Duty and Discipline

Good schools provide an orderly and safe environment. They foster a congenial environment by emphasizing duties as opposed to liberties. Effective schools don't spend a lot of time enshrining "parents' rights" or "student power." That's because a healthy school climate is the responsibility of all its participants: teachers, students, parents, and administrators alike. The school's makers can achieve this end only by drafting a clear charter of agreed-upon conduct and expectations with no tolerance for classroom disruptions. When necessary, disciplinary measures are applied fairly, swiftly, and consistently. Truancy, delinquency, and vandalism rarely trouble schools in which everyone knows the rules and has an interest in pursuing the same goals.

4. Leadership

Good schools boast assertive, on-the-spot leadership. Principals who are able administrators put the educational health of the school first when making decisions. They typically spend half of each day in hallways and classrooms, monitoring the performance of teachers and students, and they teach one or more classes a week. They select teachers carefully, infuse them with team spirit, and spend as little time as possible shuffling paper for the school board or Ministry of Education. This shunning of bureaucratic duties makes them mavericks. Sometimes to the chagrin of their superiors, these leaders spend their time matching groups of kids with the right teacher or making sure that the language needs of immigrant students have been properly met.

If, as sometimes happens, a weak principal inherits a good school, inspired teachers and/or a like-minded superintendent often fill the leadership gap. Like effective principals, able superintendents work hard to shape and direct a shared commitment to excellence. In a study of British Columbia school districts, researchers found that the best administrators made a difference "more by modelling high standards of professional conduct than by exhortation."

5. Accountability

Good schools are accountable to students and parents. The principal of an effective school explains, promptly and clearly, without academic jargon, what the school's program is, what the school expects in academic and behavioural performance, what happens to those who succeed or fail, and how performance is monitored. At good schools, programs are evaluated on the basis of pupil achievement or lack of it. If children are experiencing difficulty, the school quickly informs the parents and a plan of action is drafted. Similarly, the results of local and district-wide tests are explained and shared with parents.

6. Good Teachers

Good schools can achieve good things only with dedicated teachers. And what's a good teacher? One who believes that all children can learn and who feels he or she has failed if even one student has not obtained minimum mastery of a subject. (Education's first maxim: "What you expect, you get.") In an effective school there is a sense of collective responsibility; teachers often collaborate and share lesson plans to achieve continuity in the curriculum. Teachers welcome parents in the school and frequently employ them — not to bake cookies, but to help improve the quality of learning.

Teachers can't do it all, of course. Schools can become really effective only when all the participants — teachers, students, parents, and administrators — collectively choose the hard road. Whether a school commits itself to the noble task of teaching all children well comes down, in the end, to political will. The tools and research to do the job are not obscure nor difficult. Nor are they prohibitively expensive.

The overriding obstacle remains a school system too often managed by careerists who systematically, if unwittingly, impede reform by undermining teachers, wasting money, discouraging leadership, and driving a wedge between parents and schools.

A MODESTO PROPOSAL

In 1979 James Enochs, then the head of curriculum and instruction for Modesto schools in central California (he's now superintendent), wrote a visionary manifesto. As a radical administrator and community-minded citizen (he was an early supporter of the Cesar Chavez effort to organize grape pickers), Enochs concluded that the school system was failing because of educators' failure to remain true to the virtues of public schooling. In "The Restoration of Standards," he spelled out the problem: "Rather than be thought rigid in a period when flexibility was the highest virtue, we first relaxed our standards and then abolished them completely. We began to feel guilty and proceeded to pull up our roots and examine them for rot. Homework, honest grading, demanding courses, required courses, earned promotion — up they went and out they went. We leveled the field so that all could pass through without labor or frustration."

The appealingly destructive melody, then as now, was one that educators could never publicly acknowledge. "If there were no standardized bench marks against which to be measured," Enochs wrote, "there was no accountability. The tough, time-consuming process of monitoring — teachers monitoring students, principals monitoring teachers, superintendents monitoring principals — was lifted from our shoulders. There were fewer decisions to be made, judgements to be weighed and stands to be taken. Yes is always easier to say than no. Something called the 'affective domain' became the cloak of decency for lazy teachers and administrators. It was easier to make students feel good than to hold them accountable to the rigors of learning."

Without public prodding, government funds, or embarrassing media stories, Enochs put together a populist proposal to restore schools to their original purpose: teaching and learning. He established eight clear principles, known as the "Fourth R program," and nailed them to the door of every school in Modesto. The principles were these:

1. Public schools must define what they believe in and stand for.
2. The development of responsible adults is a task requiring community involvement. It cannot be left solely to the schools.
3. The essential tasks of a public school cannot be achieved if a disproportionate amount of time and resources must be given to police work.

4. Parents must consistently support the idea that students have responsibilities as well as rights, and the schools have an obligation to insist upon both.
5. High performance takes place in a framework of high expectations; standards without rewards and consequences are not standards at all.
6. The full responsibility for learning must be shared by both student and teacher.
7. There is nothing inherently undemocratic in requiring students to do things that are demonstrably beneficial to them.
8. In order for a program to succeed, it must be maintained for a reasonable period of time and be assured of continued support.

With these principles came a core program of basic skills from kindergarten through Grade 8: a high school graduation plan based on the mastery of specific skills and knowledge as measured by criterion-referenced tests; written codes of conduct for all grades; a character education program that underscored common values (courage, kindness, honesty, and justice); a community awards program that rewarded students who excelled in academics and citizenship; a retraining program for principals and teachers; and a homework project that actively involved parents.

To Enochs's mind, these reforms replaced "the circle of irresponsibility," or the pointless blaming of parents and students to which school administrators are prone, with a system of common civic responsibility and accountability. "We said to parents, 'You have the right to come to us and say, What will my kid know by the third grade, and how will I know that he knows it?' And we said to our employees, 'Here are the tools. Excuses are no longer valid.'"

Enochs did the right thing before it was popular and long before North America's school reform movement championed the restoration of standards. (The future, in education as in other areas of

North American life, tends to come first to California.) He also made his school board effective with sound leadership — a quality he defines as "the elevation of standards, performance, and satisfaction." He didn't solve all of his school's problems, but he did steer the entire system in the right direction. One of his more enduring and instructive mottos is a rather graphic quotation from the American poet e.e. cummings: "There are certain kinds of shit I will not eat."

James Enochs is the only school administrator in his state who doesn't belong to California's Association of School Administrators. His achievements in Modesto have rarely been repeated and in no way reflect the broader current in education. For thirty years now, the United States has been caught in a never-ending cycle of school reform that has brought with it few real changes and an even greater circle of irresponsibility. Canada has now embarked on the same fruitless cycle.

That's largely because educators, and many citizens, falsely believe that a few technical fixes — more achievement tests, better computers, teacher merit pay — can somehow energize and restore a demoralized enterprise. This piecemeal approach, a reform here and a reform there, will fail just as thoroughly in Canada as it has in the United States because it wrongly assumes that educators can fix the problem without consulting the school's other participants.

As Enochs powerfully demonstrated, effective schools cannot be sustained unless educators tackle a variety of interconnected issues together. Every school reformer in the United States knows that American schools need tougher academic curricula, better trained teachers, better testing methods, improved and literate textbooks, clear public accountability, and greater community involvement. But few states or provinces, and even fewer individual schools, have dared to address all these problems simultaneously. The lamentable consequence is that each reform fails in isolation.

This scenario is not inevitable; it didn't happen in Modesto. Even though Enochs's school district has suffered all the modern arrows of outrageous fortune (families as mobile as cars, violence as abrupt as television commercials, students as afflicted as Job), Enochs has not surrendered his vision. "We had to integrate some social services into the system. You can't teach hungry abused children. We deal with that, but then the education must begin."

Unlike many California high school graduates, whose diplomas are virtually counterfeit, Modesto students still earn a sublime document. Attendance is high, the drop-out rate low. The district has declined the latest fad — courses in self-esteem — and has no process goals. But staying effective in the difficult realms of teaching and learning is a constant struggle. Every interest group imaginable, from the religious right to the hard core of feminism, knocks at Modesto's doors seeking to shape the system in its own image. Enochs says, "It's really hard to stay on top and not go down a side street."

The citizens most actively pressing for effective schools now come from the so-called middle class, that vast fluid pool of people that includes both blue- and white-collar workers. Their populist virtues — including self-denial, thrift, steadfastness, responsibility, hard work, faith in God, and loyalty to family — helped establish the public school system a century ago by defining the meaning of democratic citizenship. In recent years, betrayed and abused by the liberal political culture, this class has chosen to make a stand by trying to regain control of the public school system.

The continent's élites tend to distrust these populist virtues. But the élites really don't seem to give a damn about the future of public schools. Having hijacked the continent's political institutions and criminally mismanaged its fiscal affairs, many political and corporate leaders would be content to see the public education system self-destruct, to be replaced by a series of morally neutral "skills centres" run by private corporations. As builders of a technological society, the élites know that they cannot really make the perfect technocrat until schools run on a corporate model. In the age of globalism, it pays to break a citizen's bonds to shared local culture, tradition, and place.

In this contest for the soul of North America, the poor and the wretched haven't the time, the energy, or the inclination to restore purpose to the continent's schools, though their allegiance has always been with populist ideals, as opposed to progressive ones. And so the movement to reform Canada's and America's schools is angrily middle class in nature and temperament. As globally orient-ed economic policies steadily diminish the power of this class, the battle for an accountable and community-minded school system will probably grow more radical. In Britain, the Tories managed to cling to power in the 1992 election largely because of the populari-ty of their school reforms, which included national standards and a national curriculum. In the United States, of course, Ross Perot began his political career by tackling school bureaucracy in Texas with the slogan "Who's in charge here?" For the next ten years, political careers in England, the United States, Australia, and Canada may well rise and fall on school issues.

THE RESTORATION OF HONESTY

More school administrators could profit from the sort of honesty that led to school reform in Modesto. "Educators have made a mess of things," Enochs wrote plainly in his revolutionary tract. "The evidence against us is overwhelming. When children are safer on the streets than in their schools, when we are spending more on vandalism than on textbooks, and when we are clothing functional illiterates in caps and gowns, the time has come to start plea bargaining. We are guilty."

No real change can take place until other North American edu-cators end the lie and admit that they have largely failed in the per-formance of their duties; that the progressive experiment has robbed children, particularly poor children, of a proper education in a democratic society; that child-centred schooling has created a generation of self-centred narcissists; and that our schools operate as fiefdoms unaccountable to the communities that fund them. No reconciliation can begin without the restoration of honesty. And no worthwhile change can take place until educators stop using the schools to promote their own welfare and careers and recognize that their first duty is to serve the public interest.

Parents, in turn, must accept that schools can do only a few things well. They must realize that whenever they treat the public school as a glorified baby-sitting service or child development centre, they change and devalue the nature of the place. If parents respect the school as an institution of teaching and learning, they will also have to embrace the full responsibility of parenting and the duties of community life. No reconciliation can begin without parents taking back what they have knowingly surrendered or had stolen from them. And no change of lasting value can occur without parents once again becoming aware of the importance of local life.

Public schools have always told us who we are and where we are going. They hold up a mirror to our collective selves. A community concerned about the quality of life will likely support a quality school, provided educators respect the community's wishes. A community that is racist will likely nurture a racist school. Parents, often engrossed in the business of consuming or abused by the robotic nature of their work, don't often demand that their schools be intelligent places of teaching and learning.

North Americans have largely failed to notice that we make our schools in the culture's likeness. When we are no longer likable as a people or a culture, our schools become unbearable places of being. And when too many citizens feel that their schools have become autonomous institutions, with missions distinct from those of the community itself, then we have entered a pre-revolutionary era.

CHAPTER FIVE

Ideas for Change

"Be ashamed to die until you have won some
victory for humanity."   HORACE MANN

M any years ago, Carl Bereiter, an educational psychologist in Toronto, observed that most school administrators really don't mind public criticism of their schools or teachers. This openness quickly evaporates, however, when the criticism includes practical solutions to the complex and deep-rooted problems suffocating the school system.

This chapter should be read not so much as a program for reform but as a collection of potentially useful ideas for teachers and parents alike. The ideas have been drawn from both conservative and liberal sources, teachers and parents, philosophers and populists. My sole aim is to promote public discourse, not silence it. Some of the thoughts presented here might well be wrong, but even in their wrong-headedness perhaps they will help us face the problems in our schools.

TELEVISION

"The arts of phantasmagoria can only stimulate a passive mind: they cannot, so far as I can see, build up habits of learning."   NORTHROP FRYE

The idiot box has no earthly message that belongs in our schools. As an instructional medium, it rarely improves student achievement and often suffocates interest. And as an educational tool, it has nothing to sell but fleeting and immediate images that promise a life largely without consequence — easy, fast, and regulated by shopping. Television blurs distinctions, hides complexities, and falsely distorts distance and time.

The research on television is unambiguous: it robs children of their imaginations and powers of concentration while slowing their metabolism. It is ultimately a harmful drug. It also exposes them to adult themes and messages that abuse the very notion of childhood. Teachers know full well that most infant couch potatoes become either passive deadbeats in the classroom or hyper hellions with "attention-deficit disorders."

Every school has an obligation to inform parents that television viewing at home is inimical to learning at school. And every parent has an obligation to inform the school that television instruction in the classroom is inimical to life at home. In future, good schools will encourage and support parents who either banish the medium from their homes or severely restrict their children's TV viewing. Good schools will also consider TV viewing in the classroom, except on rare occasions, an assault on literacy.

READING

"Anyone interested in saving humanity must first of all save the word."

JACQUES ELLUL

No subject is more integral to schooling than reading, yet no elementary subject is more poorly and irregularly taught. Despite the obfuscations of many educators, the research on reading is unequivocal. Marilyn Jager Adams, in her monumental 1990 study for the U.S. Senate, "Beginning to Read," notes: "When developed as part of a larger program of reading and writing, phonics instruction has been shown to lead to higher achievement at least in word recognition, spelling and vocabulary, at least in the primary grades and especially for economically disadvantaged and slower students."

The current enthusiasm in reading instruction, whole language, widely embraced in the 1970s, contains many useful ideas (such as making reading and writing matter right across the curriculum), but many of its practitioners do not teach phonics or spelling patterns systematically in Grade I, where these skills should be mastered.

Anita Dermer, a former elementary teacher in Scarborough, Ontario, taught phonics in a structured whole language format. She recently summarized the weakness of current reading instruction by making seven excellent points. They should be required reading in every elementary school.

I. Most children, even those with great social and economic handicaps, can be brought to a high level of reading competence by the end of senior kindergarten by any teacher with the will to do so.

2. Teaching children at this age how to read in no way interferes with the rest of the educational menu.

3. Young children are not bored by phonetics instruction. Older children (Grades 2 and up) are. That's why it should be done at an early age.

4. Many, if not most, teachers are bored by phonetics instruction. We have to admit that teaching letter-sound correspondences can be boring so that teachers, in turn, can admit that this is why they avoid it. We must also determine if many of today's primary teachers are lacking in the skills that would enable them to provide competent phonetics instruction.

5. Teachers need to distinguish between whole language and whole word teaching. The former need not include the latter (a ruinous method), although it often does. A whole language curriculum can be perfectly consistent with phonetic instruction.

6. Due to a lack of co-ordination and planning, the amount of reading and phonetics instruction varies tremendously from class to class and grade to grade, even within the same school. Most schools have unwhole and incoherent reading programs.

7. Parents and tutors all over the country provide hours of home instruction to compensate for the defects of poor reading programs. The designers of those programs then claim the achievements of those parents as their own.

A ROMANCE FOR LEARNING

"North Americans believe they are married to education but it's apparent that it's not a loving marriage. Nobody brings flowers home anymore or is even on time for dinner. Until people believe in the romance of public education our schools will not come alive again." MARILYN JAGER ADAMS

Perhaps the single greatest difference between North Americans and the people of other cultures has been the steady diminishment of our love of learning. The Asian scholar Harold Stevenson recently highlighted this sad development when he posed a challenge to American and Chinese children: "Let's say there is a wizard who will let you make a wish about anything you want. What would you wish?"

Conditioned by a media culture that daily gives the illusion that great wealth can be achieved with little effort, the American children spoke first of money, toys, and going to the moon. Only 10 per cent put doing well in school on their list. By contrast, "almost 70 per cent of the Chinese children focused their wishes on education." Shaped by Confucian beliefs that effort and diligence can shape human futures, the Chinese still appreciate the true value of careful learning and sound teaching. A long and dramatic history has taught many Europeans a similar lesson.

But here in the cradle of modernity, where memory is worth the price of salt, learning has little value. Here the teaching of a parent, master carpenter, or nurse goes largely unrecognized and unappreciated. North Americans, alienated by purposeless schools and crippled by the destructive sentiment that intellectual excellence somehow equals élitism, no longer dance a sweet dance with education.

This condition will not change until we again value learning in our homes and workplaces and remove from our schools the unheavenly burden of being the only seat of learning that matters. Only then will we begin to appreciate the school's limited but crucial role, and the special effort of children to be more than what they already are. In this endeavour, we would be wise to follow another Confucian ideal: "That the producers be many and that the mere consumers be few; that the artisan mass be energetic and the consumers temperate."

VOUCHERS AND SCHOOL CHOICE

"The term choice conveys about the same information as saying that I just ate in New York City. There are a wide variety of places to eat in New York City. Some of them are good. Some of them are okay. Some of them are dreadful. And that is my view of what we will see in a number of these choice plans."

ERIC HANUSHEK

A voucher is a piece of paper, bought with tax dollars, that guarantees parents the right to select the school their children will attend. Among policy makers in education, this free-market notion has achieved the same status that antibiotics enjoy among physicians. Simply giving parents the right to direct tax dollars to the school of their choice, however, can no more end all of North America's school problems than antibiotics can cure all illnesses.

More important, there is no evidence that vouchers can take the place of what real school reform demands: a generation of hard work. And where the voucher program has been tried — as in

Milwaukee, Wisconsin — inner-city parents have systematically taken their children out of the program. Of 341 students accepted into the program, only 86 remained the following year. Nor did students who participated show significant gains in achievement after attending private schools of their parents' choice. Transportation of students out of their communities also proved onerous and costly. The Milwaukee experiment illustrates only that, given a choice, parents would choose first to make their neighbourhood school accountable and effective.

Vouchers also pose another difficulty: where are parents to obtain reliable information about good schools? Such information, already hard to come by, would probably require the establishment of a bureaucratic clearinghouse offering a list of fuzzy variables for parents to ponder.

The advocates of vouchers also assume that private schools automatically do a better job because they are private. This is not true. Proportionally, there are just as many bad private schools as public ones. In either setting, the chance of creating an effective institution becomes more daunting each year because of the declining state of curriculum development, teacher training, textbook design, and educational philosophy.

North America's public education system definitely needs to offer more choice to parents and students but vouchers are an ineffective means to that end.

CHARTER SCHOOLS

"It is not impossible that the provision of public schools of high quality meeting a strong central consensus of the public will, together with the public provision of alternative schools for legitimate minorities, make a drift to independent schools very unlikely."
MARK HOLMES

Given that the continent's educational élites seem wedded to models of schooling that are either progressive, bland, or ineffective (and often all three together), governments must enact legislation that gives schools the power to break free of school board constraints and bureaucracy. Such legislation would enable individual public schools (and even some private schools for that matter) to become "charter" institutions that respect and uphold the fundamentals of public schooling.

These fundamentals all encompassed in a clearly worded charter would include an emphasis on high levels of academic achievement for all students and the inculcation of important civic virtues including honesty, truth, perseverance, diligence, and justice. In short, a charter school would be dedicated to getting results and respecting all the qualities that make an effective school.

By definition everyone working at a charter school would be able to choose to be there. A like-minded principal directing like-minded teachers under the watchful eye of the local community is the only sensible equation for good public schooling. As Paul Hill notes in *High Schools with Character*, good schools "are organizations with definite missions and cultures, not simply chance aggregations of individuals who happen to be assigned to the same work site."

Charter schools would also be managed on site. Although working with basic standards, curricula, and clear measures of reporting set by the province or state government, a charter school would manage its own budget, its own hiring and firing, and its own community relations. The goal of self-government in a charter school would not be to accommodate a bevy of interests but to maintain felicity to the school's basic principles.

Provided a charter school faithfully upholds the highest standards of public schooling, there is no reason it cannot be religious in character. A public school with a Catholic, Muslim, Protestant, or Ojibway student body should be able to respect and reflect the spiritual values of that community. Provided such schools do not discriminate against other religions, there is no need to fear prayer in a classroom.

Last but not least, a charter school must be wedded to the honest reporting of results. To be a charter school, in effect, the staff would be committed to regularly telling parents what a child can do, how this measures with the performance of children of the same age, what a child can't do, and what the school is doing about it and how the parents can help.

SCHOOL BOARDS

"Organizations go to seed when the people in them go to seed. And they awaken when the people awaken. The renewal of organization and societies starts with people."
                                                                JOHN W. GARDNER

Most school boards are now too big to govern wisely and too bureaucratic to spend prudently. Nearly a third of the staff in many city boards, such as Calgary, do not teach and as a result many boards, such as Toronto, now spend forty-three cents on support staff for every dollar spent in the classroom. To compound matters, school trustees have abdicated their responsibility as democratic watchdogs. Because most regard their jobs as a form of upward political mobility, they routinely acquiesce to board directors rather than represent the public will. As Horace Mann once feared, they have become "yes men" instead of "watchmen."

This depressing state of affairs will change only if boards are broken down into smaller and more accountable entities. No board truly interested in education should control more than a dozen elementary, middle, and high schools (in total) that all feed each other in the same community. This mini-board, directed by a small administrative staff (five people), could be aligned to a larger learning consortium, including Catholic, French immersion, and even private schools, which share, by special agreement, scarce resources such as buses, buildings, or experts on special education.

Unlike current boards, the new mini-board, directly governed by a group of elected trustees, would focus on teaching and learning by observing the following principles:

1. The board will have an instructional plan that tests students three or four times a year. These curriculum-based tests would be designed by teachers and an instructional leader, an individual who makes sure the tests reflect board goals. As currently practised in Matewan, a Michigan school board, a test in Grade 3 math might include twenty to thirty word problems from lessons taught in an eight-to-twelve-week period. A Grade 2 reading test might include the oral reading of a two-hundred-word passage as well as the answering of comprehension questions. This regular testing would allow teachers to change instruction in response to all student performance. Once a year, students would take a standardized achievement test as a simple independent monitor of how well everyone is performing.

2. The evaluation of the superintendent and principals would be directly linked to student learning, which can consistently be measured by curriculum-based tests. The ability of school managers is not rated by clean yards, the number of innovations adopted, and the amount of paper pushed.

3. Priorities in student learning, such as all students reading by the end of Grade 1, should set a board's budget. Too many boards now assign money to services or programs without once thinking about educational results. In many cases, the budget is set without the word education even being invoked.

4. To ensure educational goals are reached, Matewan hired instructional leaders (master teacher) for each school. Their jobs include the shaping of a consistent curriculum,

the ongoing training of teachers, the placement of students, and the co-ordination of testing. Funding for this position comes from the elimination of middle-level management. Matewan has no vice principals, curriculum specialists or coordinators.

5. Every board should have a Student Program Committee responsible for abetting and projecting student learning. Most boards now have committees for buildings, labour relations, and multiculturalism but no committee looking at what counts: how the teaching and testing of a common curriculum to all students have been served by the budget.

A board or school district that embraces these principles makes a populist declaration similar in tone to the Modesto Plan: "This is our program. This is what we expect in behaviour and academic performance. This is what happens to those who meet our standards. This is what happens to those who fail to meet our standards. Several times during the year, we'll tell you how we are doing...."

Howard Farris, a school trustee and one of the authors of Matewan's highly successful system (this small, semi-rural board near Kalamazoo offers its mixed student body one of the best educations available in Michigan), notes that most school systems have no structure in place "to ensure all student receive a quality education at every step." Real change, he adds, can't or won't happen unless the board, which symbolizes the public, seizes the day. "The widespread dissatisfaction in North America with the levels of student performance indicates that it is time for dramatic shifts in how schools conduct themselves. School boards can and should help ensure that those shifts are responsive to the needs of students and respectful of the talents and commitment of the teachers and administration."

For more details on the Matewan plan, write National Center to Improve the Tools of Educators, 805 Lincoln, Eugene, Oregon, 97401 or fax 503-346-5818.

BUREAUCRACY

"Teaching is a demanding, often back-breaking job; it should not be done with the energy left over after meetings and pointless paperwork have drained hope and faith in the enterprise."   JACQUES BARZUN

Most of the critical decisions on school policy in North America are now made by people who are neither elected nor accountable to anyone who is. As long as this bureaucracy exists, it will undermine most school reforms and thwart the public will. North Americans need to ask how many non-teaching jobs are essential to keep our schools running and why we employ more educational administrators in a typical state or province than are employed in all of western Europe.

The thousands of functionaries now pushing paper in most ministerial or state education departments are largely there to create more paper. This flow of ink prevents provincial or state ministries from doing the only two things they should be doing: curriculum development and assessment. Probably 50 to 70 per cent of the jobs in these bureaucracies could be eliminated with no noticeable effect on the schools other than profound relief.

THE RADICAL BASICS

"What is a human life worth unless it is incorporated into the lives of one's ancestors and set in an historical context?"   CICERO

In most public schools in North America, the curriculum reads like a technocratic roster of process-driven topics for self-development or problem solving. In Ontario themes appear as "Self and Society" and in British Columbia as "Social Investigations." These courses appear one curricular year only to disappear the next, like automobile models or pop stars. Subject divisions, argue the technocrats, are inconsistent with a child's view of the world; therefore, children must be allowed to construct their own meaning. Hence the incoherent and ever-changing school program.

This approach not only confines children within the walls of their own thinking patterns but also denies them access to powerful tools (such as history) for making sense of worldly mayhem. To encourage children to envelop themselves in topical and fleeting climates of self-study is ultimately to deprive them of any sense of community. As Jacques Barzun wrote, "A subject understood in common with other people is a social bond, and of a kind most desirable in a democracy."

In spite of widespread belief to the contrary, the need for common knowledge and common reference actually increases as a society becomes more pluralistic. Without a common ground and a common intellectual basis, citizens of North America can meet only as marketplace aliens who speak in television Esperanto and bumper-sticker clichés: Save the Whales. Have a Nice Day. Fight Racism.

A good core curriculum builds on three thousand years of tradition. It offers discipline and organized knowledge founded on rules and principles. It makes study successive, leads to critical thought, and eventually moulds the ability to learn on one's own. Neil Postman, the American school critic, defines the components of such an education as "history, the scientific mode of thinking, the disciplined use of language, a wide-ranging knowledge of the arts and religion and the continuity of human enterprise. It is education as an excellent corrective to the anti-historical, information-saturated, technology-loving character" of modern society.

A country that says it values education but then fails to develop a basic curriculum is intellectually bankrupt. It has behaved no differently than a government that has embraced free trade without developing an industrial policy. In each case, the possibility of attaining national, long-term goals has been thwarted by the failure to set goals. When a nation ignores its future, foreign ideas and foreign economies come to dictate national priorities.

If Canada should ever muster the courage and leadership to formulate a national curriculum and national standards, its educators will have to do something they have never done before: infuse such a program with Canadian virtues and realities. Our incoherent school programs now make it possible for students to know more about the wonders of the Amazon than the mysteries of the boreal forest. These same estranged curricula also manufacture citizens better prepared to buy indulgent lives in warm climates than to fashion prudent livelihoods in a cold one.

Last but not least, a national core curriculum must be neither teacher-centred nor learner-centred. To build a society of any lasting value, the curriculum must respect ideas, both old and new.

STANDARDS AND EVALUATION

"If mediocrity becomes a kind of censor principle setting the standard for excellence, all teachers and students at all levels suffer alike."   NORTHROP FRYE

One of the gravest and silliest assumptions that has infected educators is that standards are élitist. This modern notion, advanced in the name of egalitarianism, merely promotes the most offensive kind of discrimination, namely that ordinary people are incapable of intellectual exertion. This belief, in turn, denies most North Americans the cultural literacy necessary to have a community of self-governing citizens. In throwing out standards, writes Christopher Lasch in *The Culture of Narcissism*, educators have ensured the monopolization of educational advantages by the few and the powerful.

School standards on behaviour and essential subjects of study serve several good ends. They first let students and teachers know what is expected of them, and by doing so, inspire and guide. They are also contagious. "If an organization or group cherishes high standards, the behavior of individuals who enter it is inevitably influenced," says American educator John Gardner. "Similarly, if slovenliness infects a society, it is not easy for any member of that society to remain uninfluenced in his own behavior." A school without standards or high expectations is just a holding tank or social prison without bars.

Standards that float or change from student to student or teacher to teacher are no standards at all, but relative nonsense. "If we shape education to fit the students," writes Wendell Berry, "then we clearly can maintain no standards; we will lose the subjects and eventually will lose the students as well." Adds Berry, a university English professor who has fought numerous battles to keep standards high in his own courses, "Not only must the standards be held and upheld in common but they must also be applied fairly — that is, there must be no conditions with respect to persons or groups. There must be no discrimination for or against any person for any reason. The quality of the individual performer is the issue, not the category of the performer. The aim is to recognize, reward, and promote good work. Special pleading for 'disadvantaged groups' — whether disadvantaged by history, economics, or education — can only make it increasingly difficult for members of that group to do good work and have it recognized."

Standards have no integrity unless they are upheld with rewards and consequences. This cannot be done without regular and fair testing. Good schools have always used a battery of assessment tools that include standard examinations (writing and thinking tests that measure a student's performance against a school or national standard) and standardized tests (quick-answer multiple choice tests), which gauge a student's performance against others of the same age or grade level. Bad schools use lots of formal and informal multiple choice tests while good ones set careful exams that force students to integrate and relate ideas.

Des Dixon, a Toronto educator and author, has long argued that it is unprofessional for teachers to not test students to see if "they can read, write, speak and listen at the level of the course or grade they are about to enter!" The almost universal failure of schools to do this merely indicates how gross the betrayal of standards has become.

PRINCIPALS

"Let's face it, there is something seriously wrong with a profession in which the two most popular workshops for leaders of the profession are stress management and planning for early retirement. It does not inspire confidence to see administrators spending their time preparing for breakdown or escape. And confidence is the most important currency of leadership." JAMES ENOCHS

Principals have always set the tone of schools for better or worse. A bad leader, no matter how pleasant or nice, alienates his or her charges with uncertainty and mediocrity. In contrast, a true leader — and they are increasingly rare in the public school network — builds an ethos of high achievement within a community of singular direction.

As a true instructional leader, a principal does not shuffle paper, kowtow to obnoxious parents, or simply manage a building all day. Nor does he or she hide behind the three Bs: the board, the budget, and the bull. In contrast to managers preparing for escape or breakdown, the principal as leader spends more than half of his or her day in the hall and in classrooms directly engaging kids and teachers. Such principals often begin the day by greeting each child by name with a handshake. And they still teach a class once or twice a week because they love teaching.

In putting the academic achievement and happiness of their students first, effective principals carefully select their teachers and actively monitor their performances. While possessing little tolerance for bad teaching, they openly acknowledge excellent instructors with meaningful rewards and additional responsibilities. They also work very hard to improve the competence of struggling or inexperienced teachers by modelling the kind of skills and commitment that distinguish true professionals.

But the qualification and certification of principals rarely bears much relation to what really matters: instructional leadership. Becoming a principal these days too often means knowing how to say the political thing, take the right course, or have a background in physical education. (In some school districts, jocks make up the largest faction of people working as principals.) No school reform will succeed unless citizens and teachers focus on the role of principals as responsible leaders as opposed to technocratic managers. Insisting that school systems select and retain principals on the basis of instructional leadership and their ability to teach is a good starting point. And demanding that boards evaluate principals, if not all educational leaders, by their students' achievement would make a big difference for students.

FADS, TRENDS, AND WHIMS

"School failure is not the failure of kids, and often not the failure of teachers. It's the failure of a sick system that places more value on the whims of adults than on the obvious needs of children." SIEGFRIED ENGELMANN

Educators, as true modernists, have a fetish for innovation. Like Madonna and her ever-changing image, educational managers seem to feel compelled to remake schools again and again regardless of the consequences for children, teachers, or the integrity of local life. This compulsion to try anything new in the classroom has made schools deceptive models of change. Every change is presumably for the better, but little improvement in the quality of instruction or organization of the school actually takes place. Indeed, the quality of education, I would argue, has been in decline.

Siegfried Engelmann, an outspoken American educator, recommends that parents and teachers insist on the following abuse detectors when considering the latest policy fad:

1. No innovation or reform should be installed unless administrators and teachers have substantial reason to believe that it will result in improvement of student performance. Before the implementation of questionable practices such as "program continuity" or "continuous learning," studies with well-defined control groups must first prove that they work on a small scale and are superior to current practices. The burden of proof for programs and instructional practices in the schools rests with the school boards and administrations. If they find no evidence that the innovations will not reduce failure rates or improve reading scores, they are engaging in mindless and perhaps abusive experimentation.

2. No new approach should be installed that does not include projections about student learning. For example, a new reading series should be introduced only with the expectation that it will reduce or eliminate reading failure in Grade I for children of high, medium, or low ability. Without such stated expectations, educators cannot fairly test to see if the program has made a difference.

3. No new program or practice should be installed without frequent monitoring and comparisons with projections. In other words, educators must always ask questions: Is the new approach getting better results than the old one? What kind of impact has it had on teacher workloads? Has it compromised or reinforced existing programs?

4. Every innovation should have a back-up plan in case it fails to meet projections and makes no positive difference.

5. Schools have a moral responsibility to quickly abandon innovations that jeopardize learning in children of any ability.

6. Schools should not blame parents, children, or extraneous factors if the innovation fails. Good changes take into account the specific needs of the community. Educational reform fails for one of two reasons: it was either poorly designed (for students or teachers) or carelessly implemented. Period.

TEACHERS

"Like a good farmer, a good teacher is the trustee of a vital and delicate organism: the life of the mind in his community." WENDELL BERRY

To be a good teacher has always been hard work and will always remain so. And for far too long it has also meant toiling in isolation with few external rewards because most administrators can no more recognize a good teacher than they can write a coherent paragraph on education.

As a group, teachers rate in community value somewhat higher than journalists and lawyers but somewhat lower than good parents. As many of them honestly attest, teachers are somewhat overpaid for what they achieve and underpaid for what they endure. Self-absorbed, poorly led, and often lacking in self-criticism (criticism now equals self-esteem bashing in some quarters) the profession or trade tends to prize its contributions too smugly.

Good teachers know that effective classroom teaching cannot be reduced to technocratic problem solving, statistical research or happy students. As Jacques Barzun has so wisely observed, good teaching is a matter of overcoming a series of endless difficulties.

Like good mechanics or good doctors, teachers need to be able to choose the methods and programs for classroom work. Once they have obtained this right, then they should be held accountable for quality of instruction in their classroom. Only when teachers have this freedom will the circle of irresponsibility and the plague of mindless innovations in our schools end.

Bad teachers are notoriously difficult to get rid of. Instead of firing people who can't teach, the system either promotes or recycles them. Most trades or professions routinely dismiss 5 per cent of their members as incompetents. In teaching, the average dismissal rate is .05.[1] The reluctance of unions to prepare bad teachers for other lines of work is an abuse of children and an insult to good teachers.

TEACHER TRAINING

"Those who can, do; those who can't, teach; and those who can't teach, teach teachers."
GEORGE BERNARD SHAW

Faculties of education have made a mockery of teacher training and should perhaps be abolished. Failing that, they must assume full responsibility for the performance of their graduates. A faculty that can't consistently graduate elementary teachers who can teach 98 per cent of their children — rich, poor, or slow — how to read should lose its funding.

Instead of locating teacher training in the universities, where many professors prefer to theorize or do research, teacher training should take place in a professional centre connected to a school. After studying the subjects they want to teach, prospective teachers should learn the art and science of their trade in a two-year apprenticeship-style program. During the first year, the beginning teachers might be paired with a "mentor" and given limited teaching duties in the classroom. In the environment of a real school, beginning teachers would have to demonstrate that they know how to discipline wisely, evaluate fairly, and employ a variety of teaching tools to reach all their students. In a so-called clinical school, beginning teachers could not earn a licence to teach until they had demonstrated competence in their field as well as the critical ability to recognize when their teaching had failed.

CLASSROOM PRACTICE

"All things must be taught in due succession, and not more than one thing should be taught at one time. We should not leave any subject until it is thoroughly understood."
JOHN AMOS COMENIUS

Good teachers plan ahead and are well-organized. They gear their lessons to take their students systematically from the known to the unknown. They respect and embrace the subject being taught with enthusiasm. They expect all their students to do well. They run disciplined classrooms by methodically instilling in their students the habits and responsibilities of civility, curiosity, and dignity. They emphasize clarity of thought, content, and connections. They know that the more time students spend on math or reading, the better they will be at those skills. They monitor and pace assignments, giving frequent feedback. They encourage rather than praise and they minimize criticism. They know that a well-designed lesson will reach all students regardless of class, race, ability, or learning style. They know that some students will require more practice and others more time. They know that, in the end, good instruction overcomes all obstacles.

DIRECT INSTRUCTION

"With an eye to every consideration at once, the educator must always endeavour to connect what is to come with what has gone before."
JOHN HERBART

School reform will not be able to achieve good results in North America until direct instruction assumes its rightful and historical place in the classroom as one of the most effective tools for good teaching.

Because direct instruction is perhaps the oldest and most reliable method of instruction, progressive educators have regularly dismissed it as an anachronism. Although well-defined by the six-teenth-century father of the textbook, John Comenius, and later advocated by the German pedagogue, John Herbart, direct instruction wasn't updated and refined until a group of American educators used it to teach inner-city children in the 1970s. Their model, called Project Follow-Through, demonstrated rather conclusively that direct instruction's carefully sequenced approach to teaching resulted in superior learning in reading, math, and language development among elementary school children. In fact, direct instruction outperformed nearly a dozen child-centred methods whether based on the works of John Dewey, Sigmund Freud, or Jean Piaget. It also raised children's self-esteem by making them feel more competent and powerful.

The underlying assumptions behind direct instruction begin with the idea that all children can be taught, that the learning of basic skills and their application to high-order thinking are essential in the early grades, and that disadvantaged children must be taught at a faster rate than their middle-class peers. The success of direct instruction often depends on detailed scripted lessons, teacher supervisors, careful and continuous testing, and a proscribed method of teaching that looks like this:

1. Present an idea with clarity and economy.
2. Teach one concept at a time. This concept must admit one and only one interpretation.
3. Teach from the known (simple) to the unknown (complex).
4. Provide the student with immediate feedback.
5. Repeat concept. Practise concept.
6. Teach for generalization or what Herbart called the "many-sidedness of interest" so that the pupil transfers the idea to new situations and associations.
7. Test for mastery.

The importance of using direct instruction in the classroom has long been championed by teachers who work with poor children.

Lisa Delpit, a black educator, recently concluded that withholding direct methods from such students while exposing them only to "process" techniques "creates situations in which students ultimately find themselves held accountable for knowing a set of rules about which no one has ever directly informed them....Teachers do students no service to suggest, even implicitly, that 'product' is not important. In this country students will be judged on their product, regardless of the process they utilized to achieve it."

Progressive educators, who often advocate that students must find their own meaning, repeatedly and falsely associate lower-order skills with teacher-directed instruction. They don't realize that direct teaching sits at one end of the communication spectrum about how to present an idea while basic skills occupy a totally different continuum about what should be learned in order to become an able citizen.

Good teachers know that the dichotomy between so-called student-constructed and teacher-directed knowledge (the old understanding versus rule-following or discovery versus drill debate) is specious. Without well-organized systematic instruction, most students won't construct any meaning, high or low.[2]

DO LESS, WELL

"If the school... assumes the prerogatives normally exercised by the family, the family loses some of its motivation, authority, and competence to provide what it is designed to do." NEIL POSTMAN

Schools cannot be all things to all people. When the schools are burdened with missions to get into drug education, death therapy, planetary awareness, self-esteem sessions, day care, and multicultural pursuits, the teaching of reading, math, history, and literature inevitably suffers. By taking on such utopian missions, schools ultimately do nothing well and become places of no particular value.

This is not to say that particular schools with specific social problems such as a high incidence of teenage pregnancy should not introduce a sex education program. But there is no reason that every public school must indoctrinate its students in, say, the intricacies of gay lifestyles just because one special interest group has the clout to make it the politically correct thing to do. Such a program may make sense in communities with a preponderance of gay parents; it becomes offensive and counterproductive in communities with largely different values and needs.

The progressive crusade to use the school as a vehicle for social change and questionable agendas has only created more jobs for like-minded technocrats, whose incomes and promotions now depend on the unsuccessful treatment of social problems. It is important to recognize that after nearly thirty years of fighting racism, drugs, and poverty, North American schools have become more racist, more violent, and more illiterate in character.

North American schools can't restore standards or purpose until school administrators respect the limits of schooling, the values of their local communities, and the importance of saying no to utopian-sounding missions. Parents, for their part, must diminish their expectations of schools and stop treating them as day-care centres.

PARENTS

"There is little evidence that measures such as curricular reform, school-based management, and school choice will address, let alone solve, the biggest problem schools face: the rising number of children who come from disrupted families."

BARBARA DAFOE WHITEHEAD

In the annals of school rhetoric, "parental involvement" has become another cliché as useless as "self-esteem" and "empowerment for a democratic society." For starters, the banal term ignores the obvious:

whether for bad or good, parents have always been involved in their children's education because education begins at home.

For nearly a generation now, parents have assumed one of three different roles of school involvement. The affluent, having abandoned child rearing as an obstacle to self-expression, routinely dump ill-behaved and neglected children at the school's front door. The welfare poor, overwhelmed by the daily chaos of subsistence in broken neighbourhoods, pass onto the schools children who have dramatic material needs. And the third group, the morally committed, deliver to the schools children who value learning because as parents they have refused to surrender their children's interests and those of their community to consumer madness. This latter group frequently finds that many schools are no longer prepared for honest collaboration.

Given this parental diversity, there are only two things parents can really do to help: keep good homes and fight for better schools. Neither can guarantee good schools but together they can make them a greater likelihood, if not for this generation, then the next.

The first calling is really a matter of honouring parenting as a noble vocation. Good families put child rearing ahead of career climbing and always make sure there is one parent at home. They, too, actively monitor television watching, help with homework, and openly cherish learning. Schools know how important these activities are but rarely expect them or express thanks for them. They must do both and in doing so uphold the cultural values that strengthen families and enliven communities: commitment, obligation, responsibility, and sacrifice.

The second arena of parental work involves school politics. By forming populist groups representing all walks of life, parents can challenge the itinerant professional vandals ruining the schools. But to reassert local democratic control, which respects the limits of a school to do a few things well, will be a long and rancorous campaign. In the course of this struggle, community-minded parents will have to read the nonsense now published by education ministries and actively refute it. They will have to ignore the media because the media suspect populists and remain ill-informed about schooling. They will have to petition, not once but several times, for accurate and fair assessments of student performance. And they will have to elect trustees more interested in restoring a community of learning purpose to schools than launching a political career. To undo the damage that has been done will not be easy, but it remains the only fight worth fighting.

CHARACTER

"To deny the possibility of knowing good and bad is to suppress true openness."
ALLAN BLOOM

The idea that students will develop virtue with group-therapy-like classes in "decision making" or "moral reasoning" has been an abusive experiment on the moral life of children. It not only graduates pupils without conscience, it incredibly cultivates teachers who question the necessity of setting a good example. By routinely invading the private life of children, programs such as "values clarification" have also undermined public virtues and sought to indoctrinate the sons and daughters of ordinary people with the moral relativism of the continent's élites.

Any good program of character development, and there have been many bad ones, essentially stands on two legs. The first leg provides models of virtue in good literature, fables, myths, and histories of citizens who did the right thing at the right time. Such a program merely revives the old civic idea that certain virtues — honesty, justice, and courage — can be taught by example and practice. The second leg requires that students live these models by serving their community or school by helping those most in need. Good schools have always recognized the deeds of good citizens whether performed during or after school.

EQUALITY OF OPPORTUNITY

"A truly able person is always a threat."   ROBERT PIRSIG

Liberals have long argued that schools should allocate equal resources to equally able students, regardless of race or class, to compensate for the unequal conditions of family life. This much ballyhooed policy, however, has merely exacerbated inequalities and created ludicrous paradoxes. In Regina, Saskatchewan, for example, middle-class children receive the same access to swimming instruction as poor kids, while urban Crees get the same lessons in cross-country skiing as their white suburban counterparts. Such practices ignore the fact that most middle-class students can take swimming lessons after school on their own time; many of the inner-city poor, on the other hand, would probably never even see a pool if it weren't for a school program. As for the ski lessons, Cree students who probably don't own skis and never will are given a feel-good opportunity at the expense of more sensible lessons, such as instruction in helping elders on a reserve.

What North American schools need is not more equality but less. As a rule, writes Walter Feinberg, a school policy analyst, schools should spend the greatest resources "on those youngsters whose intellectual capacity is such that they are least likely to develop this skill on their own accord." Justice and fairness demand that North Americans not only expect more of their inner-city schools but of their denizens as well.

This does not mean blindly throwing money at schools in poor neighbourhoods. If schools with children from broken or unhealthy homes are to receive an unequally larger share of educational spending, they must consistently produce better results that would justify such unequal funding.

THE LEARNING GAP

"In education one is dealing with children in whom one has to inculcate certain habits of diligence, precision, poise (even physical poise), ability to concentrate upon specific subjects, which cannot be acquired without the mechanical repetition of disciplined and methodical acts."   ANTONIO GRAMSCI

The great abiding failure of the modern North American school is the ever-widening achievement gap between middle-class and working-class students.

Given the kind of social Darwinism that progressive thinking silently embraces, North American schools now systematically uphold the Matthew Effect: "Whoever has will be given more, and he will have an abundance. Whoever does not have, even what he has will be taken from him." (Matthew, XIII, 12).

Everyone knows that children from broken or welfare homes will likely receive less help from their parents or guardian. The damning corollary is that they also receive less teaching in school. Several studies have shown, for instance, that black or handicapped students in resource rooms receive no more teaching, and in some cases less teaching, than white and nonhandicapped peers. That's because progressive educators lower their expectations for minority students and peddle therapy instead of instruction.[3]

As long as schools offer children from poor and fractured neighbourhoods nothing more than discovery and ad-hoc curricula, the learning gap will become a sinful divide.

All students benefit from effective, intensive instruction and an intelligently organized curriculum that continuously puts ideas into a larger design, but it is the child who is the product of indifferent parenting who needs this structure the most.

BEGINNINGS AND ENDS

"Remember that schooling should begin at the beginning and not set out with hopeful endings; that it should make use of reason and ideas, but not neglect memory and practice; that it should concentrate on the rudiments so as to give a body of knowledge to some and the foundations of higher studies to others...to turn out men and women who are not wide-eyed strangers in a world of wonders."

JACQUES BARZUN

One of the philosophical tragedies of our age is a relentless confusion of ends with beginnings and vice versa. Educators illustrate the poverty of such modernist thinking by repeatedly underestimating difficulty and overestimating possibility.

The current fetish with critical thinking ("Critical and creative thinking skills and intuition are important in solving problems, making decisions and shaping new ideas," says Ontario's Common Curriculum) is a particularly good example. Having abandoned the teaching of subjects that might actually lead students to critical thoughts, such as history, educators seem to believe that they can make great minds by reducing the world's difficulties to technocratic recipes for problem solving. Without continuity or context, students are encouraged to gather isolated facts, under the ruse of some topic heading, and then solve the profound riddle of racism, say, with an ill-informed opinion.

If schools stuck to what is actually do-able — the teaching and learning of a few things — they just might graduate students who were capable of becoming critical thinkers or even original ones. But schools today can no more give students creativity and originality than they can guarantee them a great job with three months' holiday.

Sex education is another example of the schools' putting first what may or may not come last: pointed self-analysis and broader thoughtfulness about sexual behaviour in society. The flaw, of course, lies in fraudulent school programs that assume this end can be obtained with gossip, comic strips, group therapy, and direct instruction on the use of condoms.

Another beginning-end confusion is concealed in the whole idea of "holistic education," the integrating of subject matter into a roster of unrelated topics.[4] The perpetrators of this fraud forget that certain disciplines give students the power to integrate more effectively than do others, and that the synthesis of great ideas requires structured ways of thinking. For the Romans, grammar served this function: it was a tool for seeing the world clearly. For much of Western history, the Christian and Jewish faiths have helped their adherents make sense of the world. In more recent decades, history and ecology have often highlighted the connections and consequences that matter most. But the bringing together of disparate ideas represents the end of much learning, not its starting point.

SPORT

"You should pray for a sound mind in a sound body."
JUVENAL

North American schools are historically and culturally alone in believing that students can learn to think clearly without regular exercise. Most elementary schools in Canada and the United States no longer offer a daily sport program and in most high schools sport has become an option pursued only by jocks. Is it coincidence that, as these programs have eroded, the schools have fallen prey to increasing vandalism and violence?

Study after study — in France, Canada, and the United States — has shown that students who do academic work in the morning and sport and arts in the afternoon are happier, smarter, and healthier. The Japanese, as well as most Europeans, respect this truth. After every forty-minute class, Japanese students typically engage in ten wild minutes of jumping, shouting, and running.

North Americans expect their students to sit through two or three lessons before giving them a break to eat Twinkies.

Athletics programs should be a routine part of the school day. All students should be involved in sports that require the kind of effort that produces a blessed fatigue. A good sports program, like a good academic program, prepares children to handle victory and defeat, competition and co-operation, stress and play.

HIGH SCHOOLS

"The social decision to allocate educational resources preferably to those citizens who have outgrown the extraordinary learning capacity of their first four years and have not arrived at the height of their self-motivated learning, will, in retrospect, probably appear as bizarre." IVAN ILLICH

Adolescents leave high school for one of two reasons: they find it awesomely meaningless or awesomely boring. Contrary to the accepted wisdom, most drop-outs have made a wise decision; they have left large and impersonal institutions with no sense of accountability. Rather than jeopardizing their future job prospects, they're actually responding to market incentives.

To most businesses, a high school diploma nowadays is little more than a paper declaration of a student's reliability and stamina. Anyone who reads newspaper headlines or watches CNN bulletins knows that there are legions of high school graduates whose reading skills border on illiteracy and who are unable to write a grammatical sentence. Because the business community has come to discredit the diploma, students with no university ambitions know that it makes little difference whether they learn a lot or a bare minimum. Unlike businesses in Japan and in much of Europe, where high school graduates are hired mainly on the basis of academic performance, businesses in Canada and the United States tend to write off high school as a social journey and correspondingly inflate the importance of university.

A tough, lean, general high school curriculum should perhaps end after Grade 9. Students who had mastered the basic curriculum could then choose among three special programs with equally exacting standards. Students interested in pursuing university studies could enter a two-year academy-style school. Those wanting to work could enter apprenticeship programs that carried the same status as an academy-style school. And those needing something different or time off from school altogether could enter a military-style service corps in which they learned a variety of practical skills while performing valuable community work.

Changing the nature of high school in this way, and allowing students to work at a time when they need a real social role, might go some distance towards ending the societally constructed wasteland known as adolescence. The development of alternative forms of schooling and work that lead youth into adulthood, rather than keeping them prisoners of childhood, might also help break the free market's fast-food diet for young imaginations: shopping, sex, and self.

SOME SCHOOL TRUTHS

"The school of experience is no school at all, not because no one learns in it but because no one teaches. Teaching is the expedition of learning; a person who is taught learns more quickly than one who is not." B. F. SKINNER

I. Although children from well-to-do homes can partly compensate for poor schools, the disadvantaged child is doubly crippled by a weak school. Many inner-city schools simply refuse, for bureaucratic reasons, to be "a force for the good."

2. Schools can and do make a difference in spite of a child's discordant home life. Perhaps the most destructive and discriminatory belief still alive in many schools is that social disadvantage automatically leads to school failure.

3. Good schools don't treat children like welfare recipients. They give pupils real responsibility by encouraging them to help out in the cafeteria, clean the washrooms, design and plant gardens. Schools that treat students as participants rather than clients don't have much vandalism or unwanted graffiti.

4. In good schools, teachers work and plan together because they are concerned about the consistency of teaching, the ecology of group learning, and the importance of helping students make connections.

5. Schools have always been conservative places because their architects designed them to conserve certain traditions of literacy, numeracy, and wisdom. It is impossible to change the organization of schooling unless fundamental social and political change takes place outside the school.

6. Just about any school practice or methodology can be made to work in a school, provided the staff is committed to making it work.

7. Most schools committed to progressive dogma are designed for middle-class students and depend on language instruction in the home to provide the building blocks for intellectual advancement: words and their usage.

8. Just as a top-flight orchestra requires good musicians and an expert conductor, so an effective school needs dedicated teachers and the instructional leadership of a good principal.

BUSINESS

"When reformers argue over how little today's students know about their everyday world, Eurocentric and Afrocentric curricula, and how many physics courses college grad students ought to take, they miss the heartbeat of schooling; the relationship of a teacher to students over subject matter." LARRY CUBAN

In exercising their newly elevated status in North American society, business executives routinely chide schools as outdated and unaccountable organizations. At the same time, many of these same critics have pressed for schools managed by their immediate administrators ("restructuring") or have formed facile school "partnerships" with the oblique goal of having business's results-oriented savvy brush off on enterprises largely committed to the zen of processing. These corporate endeavours, whether motivated by self-interest (too many illiterate employees) or public mindedness (a democracy cannot function without a learned citizenry), often suffer from gross misunderstandings and flawed conclusions about how schools work.

Shaped by a market-driven ethos, business people often don't realize that even laudable school reforms — such as the move towards lean, self-governing administrations — won't make a substantial difference unless they include strengthened curricula, the use of effective texts, and proven classroom practices. When teachers use the same old programs to get the same ho-hum results that inspired such reforms in the first place, educators and business leaders often conclude that restructuring doesn't work. Doug Carnine, director of the National Center to Improve the Tools of Educators, a federal agency based in Oregon, notes, "If there is a range of tools available and information on their effectiveness and incentives for using tools that promote high levels of student learning, then restructuring schools might be a useful adjunct to school reform. But as long as your improvements are dragged down by poor tools all the other reforms will look like duds."

Instead of adopting schools, establishing pilot projects, or trying to decentralize school boards (all practices with questionable track records in the United States), business leaders intent on school reform should abandon the old assumptions and think like parents — which, of course, many of them are. Here are five pointers for business people interested in helping educators do a better job:

1. Be sceptical of educators.
That means being critical and informed. It means questioning the obtuse language and the shoddy research of educational experts. When educators argue that the only way to improve schools is by lowering pupil-teacher ratios, or by awarding teachers more university degrees, check the facts. There is, for example, no real relationship between expenditures on schools and student performance, nor any powerful relationship between well-degreed teachers and student achievement. This doesn't mean that large differences between schools aren't commonplace, of course, just that financing or teacher upgrading does not always explain them. "If there's a problem, educators say we have the answer and all they ever say they need is more money," says Carnine. "When you don't know what you don't know, that's a serious problem."

To help correct this reign of ignorance, business people in every state and province could help create an independent advisory council — independent, that is, of government — with the authority to monitor and analyze the productivity of schools, the growth of bureaucracies, and the proliferation of questionable fads. Right now all of the information about school performance is largely controlled (and hidden) by professional educators.

2. Act locally at the school board level.
By debating the merits of school reform in federal forums with bureaucrats unable to really change anything but their shirts,

business leaders miss the point of what schools are all about: community. One of the most important steps any business can take is to support community-education goals or populist reform groups. Although diverse, these groups share a focus on student achievement and effective schools. "By getting involved at a local level where their businesses are located," says Carnine, "business people can help communities win back control of their schools from educators." The logical focus of community action is the local school board. It is possible, economical, and realistic to reform school boards in such a way as to make student learning the primary goal.

3. Support good legislation.

Most of the tools that educators use in the classroom rarely receive the kind of quality control that car seats or children's toys are subject to. Business leaders should press for legislation that discourages fraud in our schools. The marketplace now produces educational products that sell on the basis not of what works but of what is attractive to educators. Oregon's teachers' union recently placed a "truth in labelling" bill for educational tools on its education agenda. If passed, the bill would require publishers and program developers to divulge the effectiveness and cost efficiency of their products. The notion is an excellent one and ought to be embraced by every educational jurisdiction in North America.

4. Pay attention to the quality of instruction in the workplace.

Relatively few businesses reward on-the-job learning; many don't even provide their employees with satisfactory skills training. Many businesses downplay their teaching role on the false assumption that the purpose of public schooling is job preparation. Only about a third of what goes on in high school prepares a student, in a broad sense, for a workaday life. But if schools are to succeed in their mission to produce literate and moral citizens, then the quality of learning and teaching formally established in the workplace must be improved. For that to happen, the business community must show, by its spending on training as well as by its involvement in public education, that it values a culture that values learning.

5. Respect the family.

For far too long, North American corporations have treated "family issues" as mere flotsam in the new global sea of dollars and cents. Such shortsightedness benefits neither school nor community life. As the Israeli-born social critic Amitai Etzioni notes in *The Spirit of Community*, employers typically find young people lacking in both skills and personality without realizing that such children are often the products of parents who have sacrificed their children for more income.

For employers concerned about the quality of their employees' training, honouring parents makes good economy. "A large part of what they (concerned bosses) mean is a deficiency of character and an inability to control impulses, defer gratification, and commit to the tasks at hand," writes Etzioni. "If businesses would cooperate with parents to make it easier for them to earn a living and attend to their children, the corporate payoffs would be more than social approbation: They would gain a labor force that is much better able to perform."

Corporations can make our schools stronger by actively supporting strong families. To encourage people to nurture their own children, companies should provide six months of paid leave for a newborn and another year and half of unpaid leave (two years of hands-on parenting is the bare minimum for raising healthy children). Etzioni recommends that the costs be shared by the employers of both father and mother. The government, as many European states now do, should cover six months of the unpaid leave while the family shoulders the rest of the cost.

INTERNATIONAL COMPETITIVENESS

"We must achieve the character and acquire the skills to live much poorer than we do. We must waste less. We must do more for ourselves and each other. It is either that or continue merely to think and talk about changes that we are inviting catastrophe to make."   WENDELL BERRY

Corporate leaders routinely argue that, if North American schools don't improve, our economy will lose its competitiveness. This is a half-truth. Schools make a difference to a nation's economic performance, but not a critical one. The sorry and indebted state of the North American economies is the product of ruinous economic thinking and not bad schooling. And the attempt to tie schools to purely economic goals, or to make them institutions designed to serve purely economic needs, will be just as disastrous as the "progressive" plan to have schools deliver one failed social agenda after another.

Those who demand that schools march to the rhythms of international competitiveness unwittingly demean the school's primary reason for being: the production of thoughtful citizens who know their individual rights and their community responsibilities. A business agenda for school reform, designed to improve international competitiveness, also raises another hazard: if North Americans fail to become globally competitive after the adoption of such an agenda, the credibility of public schooling becomes even weaker.

Rather than harping about global economies, the business community must accept an elementary truth: that schools, as public enterprises, should be held accountable for attaining school standards and corporations for business standards. School managers have aped the shortsighted thinking that has characterized business on this continent, but they have not directly affected an economy that has never placed a premium on literacy or learning.

In arguing for school reform in the name of international competitiveness, business leaders give genuine school problems an abstract and false description. No school problem is truly "global," just as no environmental crisis is truly "planetary." Schools can no more make a country internationally competitive than they can end poverty. But if the schools uphold school standards and produce informed, literate, and thoughtful citizens, then the local community will flourish and with it, eventually, the larger economy. Small business leaders, rooted in the idea of community, understand this indirect connection better than do corporate titans wedded to their increasingly global networks.

School reform in North America should be aimed at preparing its citizens not for global economies hell-bent on growth but for local economies respectful of local life. This implies, among other things, teaching all North Americans to lower their material expectations before our economic habits bring upon our children painful judgements Job himself could scarcely bear.

In our schools, as in our companies, the salient issue is not a lack of respect for economic competitiveness but lack of leadership, long-term direction, and farsighted priorities.

MULTICULTURALISM

"If I am a newcomer to your country, why teach me about my ancestors?... Teach me about cowboys and Indians; I should know that tragedies created the country that will create me."
RICHARD RODRIGUEZ

Enshrining multiculturalism in our schools is another sure recipe for fragmenting the public school. By catering to the particular whims of particular groups, whether gays or native Indians or Hispanics or other "neglected minorities," educators inevitably give children unequal and uncommon curricula. In doing so they deny the central virtue of a public school: the sharing of a common and rich heritage animated by many cultures. Ironically, separate and relative programs for different students pointedly tell the majority that these minorities don't matter and probably don't belong in any common discourse. History documents rather boldly that separatist curricula can encourage yesterday's victims to become tomorrow's executioners.

The current crusade for multicultural education (the "tolerance for diversity" bandwagon) is also philosophically bankrupt. It ignores the uncomfortable truth that most multicultural policies were born out of an attempt to bribe new immigrants to support particular political parties. The politically correct call for tolerance also ignores older and more powerful social precepts such as acceptance and forgiveness. "Tolerance is the attitude of those who don't really believe in anything," says Christopher Lasch. Public schools cannot survive without specific values and a strong belief in community. "To say that all beliefs are equally deserving of tolerance is to admit they are all equally unimportant," says Lasch.

Public schools cannot provide the seeds of common discourse by emphasizing cultural differences, severing memory, dismantling national culture, promoting cultural relativism, or replacing the study of popular history with therapeutic programs designed to heighten the self-esteem of particular minority groups. Education that is tribal simply cannot be public.

THE FUTURE

"We assume that with money and know-how everything desirable can be achieved by short-cuts and accelerated programmes. We do not respect knowledge; we exploit it."
                                                                    HILDA NEATBY

If alliances of parents and teachers cannot restore common sense and common purpose to public schools, then the institution will continue to fall to pieces. In this regard, the worst enemy of the public school system remains its quisling-like managers. For the more they resist populist calls for accountable governance, basic curricula, character development, and good teaching, the more they invite a future that will not include public schools. "It is obvious," wrote Horace Mann nearly a century ago, "that neglectful school committees, incompetent teachers and an indifferent public may go on, degrading each other, until the noble system of free schools shall be abandoned by a people, so self-abased as to be unconscious of their abasement." We have reached this point so insidiously that even most school administrators don't realize the barbarians are now within the gates or that they, in many cases, are the barbarians.

The key power taking advantage of this tragedy is also its central author: technological society. Having already pushed free market individualism to its limits in the public schools, the technological imperative has skilfully begun to erect the public school's logical replacement: independent contract-learning systems. Throughout North America, firms have begun to establish centres where dissatisfied parents can sign up their children for computer-assisted instruction in math or reading. The unwritten object of these programs is what Neil Postman aptly calls the technocrat's ideal — "a person with no commitment and no point of view but with plenty of marketable skills." But if schools cannot develop basic skills in reading, writing, and math within the context of shaping democratic citizens, then parents will and should seek alternatives wherever they can find them.

Sometimes the firms most actively erasing common purpose are really public schools that remain public in name only. The Vancouver school board, for instance, has established Virtual High, "tomorrow's secondary school, today." Devoted to modernism and all of its biases, the school will allow students to decide what they want to learn and to teach themselves or contract experts to do so. Laptop computers and modems will be the main learning tools. "We think kids are brighter than we perceive them," said co-founder Michael Maser recently in the *Vancouver Sun*. "So we turn the learning focus over to them." In a culture devoted to self-interest, this is an appealing credo to adolescents. Confessed one recent enroller in Virtual High: "I'm not going back to a [traditional] public school. I want to learn skills that are valuable to me." But when the goal of any school, college, or university becomes solely that of equipping people to fulfil private ambitions, then the justification for public support withers away.

Perhaps the best-known manifestation of this trend is Chris Whittle's Edison Project. The Tennessee businessman, notorious for his selling of commercial-driven current affairs shows to American schools, proposes the creation of one hundred high-tech "campuses" that could educate 200,000 students from kindergarten to Grade 12. To set up the Edison Project by 1996, Whittle needs to raise $3 billion worth of private capital. Whether or not such a grand scheme is feasible, Whittle's ambitions illustrate future possibilities if not directions.[5] When fast-food restaurants and computer companies already run their own so-called universities, there's little to stop Whittle and company from running schools. Education Alternatives Inc., a Minneapolis company, has already done so with mixed success in Florida and New Jersey.

The social trends favouring these kinds of contractual high-tech arrangements are the same ones that have battered the school system: the family's loss of rootedness, our community's surrender of purpose, the culture's abandonment of any provisional morality, and government's enslavement to debt. North America has chosen to make itself vulnerable to the unwanted and undesirable. Aristotle once wrote that since the whole city has one end, "it is manifest that education should be one and the same for all." Modern society has inverted this republican proposition: since technology has an efficient and marketable end for every individual, education must be private and different for all. This strange and disquieting future now stalks our schools, promising uncommon destinies far from the school ideal of building wise countenance and stout heart.

Appendices

This appendix has been selected to be used as a resource guide for parents and teachers. Some of the passages are short and some long, but all reflect clear thinking about schooling.

Although a few selections directly complement the book (Marilyn Jager Adams's research on reading, for example), many passages such as Carl Kline's essay on school proofing stand alone as important statements.

APPENDIX I

Marilyn Jager Adams, a fiery Boston educator, produced a remarkably comprehensive study on beginning reading for the U.S. Senate in 1990. Although her highly acclaimed and very readable report did not end the debate on reading instruction (many educators still refuse to read it), it emphasized the critical importance of teaching phonics regardless of the kind of method a teacher is philosophically wedded to. Here, then, are the conclusions of her summary report. (For information on how to order the summary or book form of *Beginning to Read: Thinking and Learning about Print*, phone the Center for the Study of Reading: 217-244-4083.)

BEGINNING TO READ:

THINKING AND LEARNING ABOUT PRINT

by Marilyn Jager Adams

A SUMMARY

Prepared by
Steven A. Stahl
Jean Osborn
Fran Lehr

Center for the Study of Reading
The Reading Research and Education Center
University of Illinois at Urbana-Champaign

CONCLUSIONS

Effective reading instruction depends not only on what one does, but also on the depth and quality of the understandings by which it is guided. An analogous statement can be made for the following conclusions. They are valuable only with an understanding of the processes and considerations on which they are based.

Predictors of Reading Acquisition

- Performance on perceptual tests do not involve linguistic skills or facility with print does not appear to relate to reading success.
- Letter recognition skills are strong predictors of reading success. It is not simply the accuracy with which children can name letters that gives them an advantage in learning to read, it is their basic familiarity with the letters—though this is typically reflected in the ease with which they can name them.
- Awareness that spoken language is composed of phonemes is an extremely important predictor of success in learning to read.
- Children's general awareness of the nature and functions of print is a strong index of their readiness to learn to read.

Before Formal Instruction Begins

- The single most important activity for building the knowledge and skills eventually required for reading appears to be reading aloud to children regularly and interactively.
- Children learn a great deal about both the nature and function of print through thoughtful interactions with adults.
- Language experience activities and the use of big books are excellent means of establishing print awareness (although they are less useful as primary vehicles for reading instruction itself).
- Children recognize a variety of environmental print that they encounter day to day, but environmental print does not seem to contribute to reading success unless a child has first begun to learn about the individual letters.
- Learning to recognize and discriminate the shapes of letters is a difficult process requiring support and encouragement. Ideally, letter knowledge should be well established before children reach first grade.
- Among preschool children in the United States who learn about letters at home, it is typically the names of the letters that are learned first, often through the alphabet song. Learning about their shapes comes later, and their sounds, later still.
- Some children have difficulty conceiving of spoken language as consisting of individual words. The concept of "word" can be developed easily, though, through exposure to written text or through direct instruction. Children should also be helped to appreciate the relationship between the lengths of spoken and written words.

- Activities designed to develop young children's awareness of words, syllables, and phonemes significantly increase their later success in learning to read and write. The impact of phonemic training on reading acquisition is especially strong when phonemes are taught together with the letters by which they are represented.
- Early encouragement of printing is both a way of developing letter recognition skills and enabling children to write independently.

Beginning to Read

- Approaches in which systematic code instruction is included along with the reading of meaningful connected text result in superior reading achievement overall, for both low-readiness and better prepared students.
- Programs for all children, good and poor readers alike, should strive to maintain an appropriate balance between phonics activities and the reading and appreciation of informative and engaging texts.
- Matching children to different instructional programs based on dominant perceptual modality or styles does not appear to improve the efficacy of instruction.
- Writing and spelling activities, in general, are a means of developing and reinforcing knowledge of spelling and spelling-sound patterns.
- Independent writing activities are a means of developing children's deeper appreciation of the nature of text and its comprehension.
- The texts that children read influence the reading abilities they develop. Texts that contain a higher proportion of decodable words promote independent word recognition growth. As reflected by their writing, children also absorb the syntax, vocabulary, and conceptual structures of the texts they read.

Phonics Instruction

- Phonics instruction is not only a means of teaching children to sound words out, but also of directing their attention to the spellings of words.
- To maximize word recognition growth, the wording of children's early texts should be carefully coordinated with the content and schedule of phonics lessons.
- The ability to recognize letters is extremely important to the development of word recognition.
- For children with little letter knowledge on entry to school, current learning theory suggests it is unwise to try to teach both upper case and lower

case forms of all twenty-six letters at once. For children who do not know letter names on school entry, special care should be taken to avoid confusion of names and sounds.

- Classroom encouragement of invented spellings is a promising approach toward the development of phonemic awareness and knowledge of spelling patterns.
- The learning of regular spelling patterns and their phonic significance may be hastened through methodical use of onsets and rimes.
- Because most phonemes cannot be pronounced without a vowel, many programs avoid or limit the use of isolated phonemes in their instruction. This practice often leads to potentially confusing instruction. The advantages of asking students to articulate phonemes in isolation outweigh the disadvantages.
- Because children have special difficulty analyzing the phonemic structure of words, reading programs should include explicit instruction in blending.
- Reliance on special terminology may subvert the purpose of the lessons in which it occurs.
- Although rules and generalizations cannot substitute for direct practice with the words to which they pertain, they may be useful for either directing students' attention to a particular spelling pattern, or providing strategies for coping with difficult decoding patterns.
- Phonic rules and generalizations are, at best, of temporary value. Once a child has learned to read the spellings to which they pertain, they are superfluous.

Beyond the Basics
- Children should be given as much opportunity and encouragement as possible to practice their reading. Beyond the basics, children's reading facility, as well as their vocabulary and conceptual growth, depends strongly on the amount of text they read.
- Reading comprehension depends on the ability to perceive words relatively quickly and effortlessly.
- Reading comprehension also depends on the conviction that text is meant to be understood and thought about.
- To maximize achievement, children should be given texts that they can read orally with 90% to 95% accuracy.
- Given that a text is at an appropriate level of difficulty, it is preferable that children be encouraged *not* to skip words that are difficult for them.

Instead, they should be encouraged to take the time to study a word, and then reread the entire sentence or phrase in which it appears.

- Repeated readings of text are found to produce marked improvement in children's word recognition, fluency, and comprehension.
- Encouraging children to learn to spell words correctly is important because spelling knowledge directly affects their reading ability.

Appendix 2

C arl Kline is a retired Vancouver psychiatrist who spent a large part of his career working with pupils with learning difficulties. After treating more than four thousand students, he concluded that most of their problems were the products of bad teaching or "teaching disabilities" as opposed to "learning disabilities." For a number of years he and his wife, Carolyn, have advocated that parents "school proof" their children by teaching them how to read. As long-time Democrats and community activists (Carl's opposition to the Vietnam War brought his family to Vancouver in 1969), they wrote the following essay in 1989.

SCHOOLPROOFING

By Carolyn Lacey Kline with Carl L. Kline, M.D., F.R.C.P.(C)

SchoolProofing—our prescription for protecting children from the devastating effects of reading failure. Like the term from which we've coined the phrase, "streetproofing," we see this as an intervention program to safeguard children. Streetproofing incorporates a training program to guard potential young victims against certain hazards of urban life. SchoolProofing, as we visualize it, would protect beginning students against the confusion and humiliation they too often experience as the result of typical first grade reading instruction.

The reluctance of educators to learn from impressive longitudinal studies on reading instruction continues to puzzle us. The research findings clearly demonstrate the advantages of teaching children to read through intensive, explicit, multi-sensory phonics; yet teachers, heavily influenced by the International Reading Association and the National Council of Teachers of English, emphasize various versions of the whole word/whole language approach. Phonics instruction, at best, is gradual and haphazard. Accuracy is sacrificed for what they call "comprehension," but obviously true comprehension is impossible when words are guessed at or misread. Stories are meaningless when the child reads "goat" for "garden" and "house" for "holiday." (Meticulous research by Dr. Patrick Groff, prolific contributor to The Reading Informer and The Sounds of Reading, provides invaluable information about the prevalence and the dangers of "smorgasbord" reading instruction with a bit of everything on the plate except structured phonics.)

Several years ago a well-known spokesman for the whole-word/whole-phrase/whole language approach stated in a keynote address to teachers: "It doesn't matter if a child reads 'cat' for 'kitty'—he has got the concept, and that's what's important. If he reads 'cake' for 'candy,' you ask, 'Does that make sense? Look at the picture. What does it tell you?'" At best this reduces reading to a word memorization game from which the language-sensitive child might eventually construct his own set of rules and generalizations. At worst it becomes an ongoing guessing activity that dooms the child to academic underachievement. A phonics-confident child would KNOW that c-a-t could never spell "kitty." And certainly the average parent rightly suspects (but often is too intimidated to say) that failure to teach intensive letter-sound associations and letter-patterns in structured integrated reading/spelling lessons does not make much sense.

Present teaching methods typically make the acquisition of reading an unnecessarily difficult, complicated job. Any phonics component, too little and too late, tends to be unrelated to spelling and written expressive language, skills that are invaluable in reinforcing an understanding of letter-sound association and more advanced aspects such as syllabication.

Secondary school teachers don't turn their chemistry students loose in the lab and tell them to try out the equipment and make something. First the students must learn some specialized vocabulary and certain fundamentals. Teaching the basics also is the appropriate, logical way to introduce the child to reading. It is after the primary decoding-encoding skills are learned that the child is truly liberated to read with pleasure and self-confidence anything that interests him.

To return to the concept of SchoolProofing, we contend that teaching the young child the basics BEFORE he gets to school provides the best insurance against reading failure. Once the child understands that words say what they do because of their letters and the organization of those letters, and not because of some arbitrary decision on the part of the teacher or because of the illustrations in the book, the teaching methodology in place in his school any particular year will not unduly confuse him. (Actually, the student called upon by the grade one teacher to demonstrate reading skills for visitors most often is a child who entered grade one knowing phonics and able to read.)

After thirty-five years of working with school children in the United States and Canada who are non-readers, poor readers, and word-guessers, we have lost faith in the school system. The new approach they introduce every few years (usually in British Columbia at least, as imports from California and Arizona) turns out to be a catchy version of old methods that have left illiterates in their wake. Such programmes as neurological impress, language experience, learn-through-exposure to roomfuls of colorful books (osmosis?) and so forth. Mitford M. Mathew's historical survey of reading methods, Teaching to Read, provides fascinating insight into the cyclical nature of reading instruction. For example, he quotes Fredric Gedike writing in 1779: "It is neither necessary nor useful to begin learning to read with a knowledge of the individual letters, but it is not only far more pleasant but also far more useful for the child if it learns to read entire words at once, because this is the way it will be occupied immediately with whole ideas..." Since this is a theme that keeps recurring among educators, it surely must sound familiar to most adults today.

Perhaps the method most in use at this time, certainly in British Columbia, is the whole language approach which seems based upon that the acquisition of reading skills should come as naturally as the acquisition of spoken language. Although this is an idea that has been attacked by authorities in many disciplines as lacking validity, it keeps rising to the surface over and over again. At the conclusion of his survey, Mitford Mathews comes out strongly in favour of teaching children to read through intensive, structured phonics, and he quotes University of Michigan's Professor Selma

Fraiberg with approval: "Those systems which employ a phonics approach from the start have a very small percentage of reading failures even among children with I.Q.'s in the eighties and nineties."

Unfortunately, as we've learned from long experience, there's little chance that professional educators and teachers will soon convert to this simple methodology. That's why we urge a campaign to SchoolProof children before they enter first grade. Teach them letter-sounds, letter-generalizations, and how to use this information in reading and writing. Teach them in a structured programme, limiting reading and spelling in the first phase to a phonetically controlled vocabulary. And suddenly, the whole world of literature is theirs to enjoy and share.

This is what we mean by SchoolProofing: to teach reading to the preschooler—your own, or, as a volunteer, the children of others. In providing this help at a critical time, before failure sets in, you will be sparing children the emotional trauma that too often results from classroom instruction; and you will be providing not only the child but yourself with a wonderfully satisfying, exciting experience.

Our early experience in the 1950s with reading problems was limited to psychiatric referrals of disturbed children and adolescents who turned out to have a primary reading disability (developmental dyslexia). We soon learned that appropriate treatment was not psychiatric but educational: intensive remediation employing explicit phonics with multisensory reinforcement. By necessity this led to our involvement in training remedial therapists, including parents working with their own children. While challenging, this project was not as formidable as we had first anticipated, and the success rate was impressive.

In those days there was little publicity about illiteracy in the schools, and we did not realize that a large number of non-dyslexic children also were failing to learn to read and spell. Not surprisingly, many such children were referred to us, and for them we advocated the same intensive phonics approach that had proven so effective in treating dyslexia. However, their progress was dramatically faster than that achieved by the dyslexic children, and we soon became convinced that basic phonics should be used for teaching all children to read and spell.

Today's parents are better informed about the high incidence of reading problems, and they are increasingly uneasy about the way their children are being taught. Yet they understandably feel inadequately prepared to assume the responsibility for home instruction. Often they have read warnings by educators about the dangers of early reading instruction (especially by non-professionals), and they don't want to risk inadvertently CAUSING a reading problem.

They can relax. Learning to schoolproof children is not difficult. In fact, the early Greeks, who taught reading exclusively through intensive phonics, typically turned the job over to their slaves because it was considered a simple and undemanding task. As far as any detrimental result from early teaching is concerned, there is evidence that preschoolers are at the optimal age for such instruction. (The Montessori schools, which traditionally have encouraged very early writing/reading skills, offer highly visible proof.) The school population at emotional risk because of academically related problems is not composed of those children who enter first grade knowing how to read. Rather, it is composed of those children who fail to learn due to poor teaching methodology. In fact, most psychiatrists agree that reading disability itself is the leading cause of emotional problems in children and adolescents in North America.

The easiest way for parents to learn how to teach their pre-schoolers to read is through getting personal training themselves. This sometimes is available through phonics workshops such as those sponsored by the Reading Reform Foundation experts. When such instruction is not available, parents can learn through independent study. We recommend the following approach for home-schoolproofing:

STEP ONE: Read WHY JOHNNY CAN'T READ and WHY JOHNNY STILL CAN'T READ by Rudolf Flesch. These provide excellent insight into the problems as they exist in the schools, and offer well-researched information about the advantages of intensive basic phonics instruction. (Reading Reform Foundation, 615 Lafayette, Steilacoom, Washington 98388. (206)-588-3436. [also at many bookstores—Ed.])

STEP TWO: Purchase THE ACTION ALPHABET by Anne Rushworth. We consider this to be an indispensable beginner's program for teaching the correct printing of the alphabet, common sounds for each letter, mnemonic devices for reinforcing letter-sounds, with a multisensory approach. (Artel Educational Resources Ltd., 109 8474 Ontario Street, Vancouver, B.C. V5X 3E8. (604)-435-4949 Bus., (604)-435-1955 Fax., $7.25 Canadian.)

STEP THREE: Purchase RECIPE FOR READING by Nina Traub. This is a complete phonics program composed of the text, a manual, and twenty-one story books. It uses a multisensory approach, is easy to follow, and has great appeal for children. (Basic Educational Books, 420 Bell Street, Edmonds, Washington 98020. (206)-775-4710. $65.28 U.S., about $75.70 Canadian.)

These additional suggestions will be helpful to parents who wish to teach their pre-schoolers:

1) Work on a one-to-one basis.
2) Limit the session to 30-45 minutes with a mid-way break, four or five times weekly.
3) Choose a quiet area free of disruptions and away from other family members.
4) Until the "code" is learned, work only with phonetically controlled reading material (composed of letter-sound associations that the child has learned).
5) Always use part of the lesson time for dictation of phonetically regular words within the child's capabilities.
6) Discourage guessing.
7) Avoid the punishment-reward syndrome.

Even the most enthusiastic children will have an occasional difficult day, often for no obvious reason. At such times the materials should be put away quietly with a casual comment such as "We'll do some more reading tomorrow." Sometimes children get stuck on a plateau or even regress. If that occurs, "vacation time" has arrived. Resumption of the lessons after a few weeks' holiday typically is marked by good progress once again.

Pre-schoolers who are taught by their parents obviously will have varying degrees of success. But in acquiring a good understanding of the letter-sound system and some level of real reading competency, they will have developed an invaluable PHILOSOPHY of reading. Once children have mastered the phonics code and have acquired good blending skills, the exciting world of books is theirs to explore and savour. In contrast, children being taught by the whole word or whole language approach have only a limited access to printed words and often remain poor spellers for life.

Recently the mother of a schoolproofed first grade boy asked him if he was glad she had taught him to read last year. He said, "Sure. Two reasons: Some of the big kids in my school don't even know how—even one twelve-year-old boy, but I don't have to worry about learning. And the best thing:

At night, after you read me a story and send me to bed, I can turn on my light and keep on reading."

That little boy's mother has the satisfaction of knowing that school-proofing works. It has immunized her son against reading failure, and it has opened the wide world of books to his eager young eyes. He understands how letters make words and how words make sentences that turn into wonderful books for him to enjoy (even AFTER he's been sent to bed). Until schools abandon their present whole word/whole language programs and teach reading through intensive, explicit phonics, we hope that all parents will emulate this child's mother and schoolproof their pre-schoolers at home. It works.

Reprinted with the permission of Carolyn and Carl Kline

Appendix 3

TRYING TO TEACH

In 1993 the Alberta Teachers' Association (ATA) broke a long silence in the trade by publishing a revolutionary report that addressed the whole subject of classroom practice. (Teachers' unions have historically kept their nose to salary and pension grindstones.) Gut-wrenching and bluntly honest, the study documents the bad effects of technocratic meddling (a plethora of unrelated school reforms) on schools, pupils, and teachers. It is based on eloquent submissions from more than two hundred staff rooms in Alberta.

I have selected comments on "trends and observations," integration, and the report's unorthodox conclusions. The full study (27 pages) can be obtained by phoning: (403) 453-2411.

II WHAT IS THE PRESENT SITUATION?

A. Overview
In general, two broad views on "trends and innovations" and their combined effects seem to emerge: responses tended to fall on a continuum between these two views:

View One: *There is no overall plan: the situation is chaotic and often contradictory.* This view sees different levels of government imposing conflicting expectations (which are inadequately explained or defined), and identifies contradictions between such developments as program continuity and increased external testing, or between integration and results-based curriculum. An analogy is made to a medical situation: What if a patient were to see one doctor for a foot problem, another specialist for a throat infection, another for high blood pressure and so on. If each doctor, acting independently of the others, prescribed a medication, should we be surprised that the patient suffers from a drug interaction?

View Two: *There is no overall plan, and it will dramatically change our classrooms and teaching.* Some of the newer junior high schools in our larger urban school districts are the harbingers for what is to come in education in general, according to this view. In one such school, "grades" have been abandoned; students from "year" 7, 8 and 9 are grouped together in "teams." Teachers "are considered learning coaches"; "subject specialists" are no longer utilized; a teacher works with the students in almost all subjects. Students with special needs (physical, mental, learning, behavioral) are integrated into the classroom; there is a wide range of ability among the rest of the class. Learning is "customized and personalized for each student"; each works at his or her own rate. Diagnostic tests indicate the "level" for each student in each subject area, and the extent to which "results" have been achieved. Each student has an "individual pupil program"; student progress is also reflected in (and assessed through) "portfolios." Teachers emphasize cooperative learning, and students constantly make use of educational technology.

Regardless of whether there is or is not a clear overall plan, there is no doubt that important changes are taking place; they are having a major impact, and their consequences must be examined and assessed. In addition, it is obvious that the profession needs to have a very clear view of where education should be headed, if teachers hope to influence the direction of change, and if teachers' voices are to be heard.... However, a number of points need to be made.

1. Some developments may be good in theory, but, through lack of support or faulty implementation, may be unsound in practice as a result. (Many submissions raised integration of special needs students in this context.)
2. Some developments may be very desirable to an extent, but may be undesirable or unworkable in a more extreme form. (Because

full integration is good for some students, is it necessarily best
for all students in all circumstances? If portfolios are effective
in some settings, does that mean they should be mandated in all
classrooms at all levels?)
3. Some development may be desirable in themselves, but may be
unworkable when combined with other changes that are occur-
ring at the same time. (For example, the combined effect of
integration, individualization, program continuity and
increased external testing has led some elementary teachers to
state that they simply can no longer do their jobs.)

B. Integration

Without doubt, the specific development causing the greatest amount of
concern among teachers is "integration." The submissions on this topic
were the most in-depth and passionate, and clearly displayed the frustration
felt by teachers.

There are some disagreements over the meaning of the term.
"Mainstreaming" is used less often; some increasingly prefer the term
"inclusive education." However, the principles seem to be summed up in
the ATA Special Education Council's definition of integration as "the practice of educating children with special needs in the regular classroom in
their neighbourhood school with their non-handicapped same-aged peers."

Integration, in some form, is an increasing reality in many Alberta classrooms, and is viewed by many as "the educational placement of first
choice." Some expressed absolute support for its goals:

- All children have, by law, a right to education... To isolate any child
because we fail to understand their needs is our failure and our system's
failure. Our nation needs to become more tolerant of differences, cultural
or developmental. What better place than a classroom to learn that tolerance? What better person than a teacher to model tolerance, acceptance
and the value of diversity?
- The value and success of integration depends greatly upon what is considered most important in education. The rights of an individual, his
value to society and the maturity of a society to accept all its members
are increasingly being stressed in Canada. This makes integration an
important goal for Canadians. I strongly encourage it.

But in general, the submissions overwhelmingly expressed a deep concern on the part of many teachers that in too many cases the process is not working, and is in fact creating educationally unsound situations.

In many instances, teachers expressed support for the principles of integration, but identified critical problems in its implementation:

- I am wholeheartedly in favor of integration of students with special needs. My experience, however, has led me to believe that some integration programs are in fact abandonment or submersion programs.
- For the most part we agree with the philosophy of integration, however, schools must have adequate resources to meet the needs of the integrated students without detracting from the needs of regular program students. These resources should include funding, programming, consulting services and material resources.

Others focused more directly on the lack of necessary support:

- Integration of students with special needs in our school means "dumping" the child in a regular classroom with no aide, no extra time to work with the child or prepare and no professional resources to support us.
- This "dumping" of special needs students without aides, without consulting services, without necessary resources and without inservicing has added stress, frustration and work on the teacher. It has created a negative effect on the other students and is not meeting the educational requirements of the special needs child.

Some maintain that it is a good idea for some students, but not necessarily for all:

- An example is a dependent handicapped autistic 11-year-old boy who was integrated in my Junior Adaptation classroom. He was functioning at about a 20-month-old level, with an approximate IQ of 25-30. Although appropriate programs focusing on his level of functioning were available and recommended, his parents adamantly decided it would be better for him to be integrated. The boy had also been integrated in our school for the two previous years. The cost of educating him, taking into account aide time, teacher time and consultant's time, was between $25,000 to $30,000 per year. In short, it cost between $75,000 to $90,000 to educate him during the three years that he was at our school. Had he been in an ability appropriate program he would not have required a full-time aide and would have cost far less money. Monetary cost was not the only "cost" of this integration. It reduced the overall preparation time that I had for the other students' program because I was responsible for setting up and monitoring two *distinctly* different programs. The students additionally "lost out" in learning through the number of disturbances created by this student. He would frequently cry out, make whimpering sounds, bolt across the room, lie upon the floor and giggle, and attempt to masturbate. How does this promote excellence in education?

Others point to the problems related to the lack of essential training for "regular" teachers:

• Up until now, it seems that we needed highly trained special needs teachers to assess these students and develop individual programs specifically suited to each student's needs. These teachers needed special university training to learn how to do this. Once in the workplace, they also needed low numbers of students under their care due to the great time factor required to plan individual programs and the need to deliver these programs on a one-to-one basis. Now someone is trying to tell us that every teacher can do this even if they have no training, no time, and all the other regular students to still plan and mark for as well. This is absolutely ridiculous and I fail to see how anyone can benefit.

The lack of inservice training was also an item of concern:

• Teachers need support and inservicing for this to succeed. Even though these students can be generally included in the main program instruction, they do have special needs that have to be addressed. Teachers need help with setting up programs—academic and social.

Some focused on the impact of these practices on "regular" students:

• It's difficult to understand why five years ago we hired specialized special needs teachers to work with special needs students in small groups. Now suddenly, we are informed a regular classroom teacher can handle 25 to 30 regular students as well as any number of special needs students in one classroom. My concern is what is going to happen to the average and above average student. Obviously, with the time required designing new programs and administering these, and all of this done by teachers unfamiliar with the needs of a special student, the average student will get less of the teacher's time. I wonder how parents of average children feel about the teacher's lack of time to help their children?

Others felt that the situation has resulted in a failure to meet the needs of either "special needs" or "regular" students:

• Many of the teachers feel that without extra help in the classroom, this trend in education is not having a positive effect on any of the students involved. We are not able to spend enough time with these students to create a significant difference in their learning. Yet, we are spending more time with them and neglecting our "regular" students to an extent that we feel that they are suffering. This, I'm sure, you have heard before....

Some questioned whether some aspects of integration were reasonable in theory or in practice:

• Many teachers are not qualified or interested in teaching special needs students (especially emotionally disturbed and severely handicapped). I believe we should have that choice. My doctor is a GP and excellent at her job. She does not, however, perform brain surgery, but has the option of referring these special needs to a specialist. Does that make her a poor doctor? My daughter is a special needs child (IQ=77). She spent six years in [one school system] in tears and frustration, being taunted and picked on because she was "stupid." Then [another] board (after an eight-week enrolment time) placed her in a special class—integrated wherever she could cope. Her attitude has completely turned around; she feels safe to risk and is making excellent progress. Integration must be best for teacher, special needs child and the rest of the class (who often suffer because special needs children take up teachers' time) or it is an exercise in futility....

A. Recommendations

The committee makes the following recommendations:

Recommendation 1 That a comprehensive position on public education and professional practice be developed, based on the following foundation:

I. A significant reduction in the expectations placed on public education, based on clear and deliberate choices.

2. Elimination of contradictory expectations, in a clear statement of realistic, achievable goals and directions.

3. Recognition and enhancement of professionalism and of teachers' rights to make choices and judgments in the light of their training, experience, expertise, and needs and interests of their students (with particular reference to Sections 1, 3 and 4 of the *Declaration of Rights and Responsibilities for Teachers*[1]).

4. Provision of the resources to allow teachers to refine and perfect instructional techniques.

5. Efficient organization of schools to recognize the constraints of group instruction and the reasonable limits to individualization.

6. Provision of necessary supports for all introduced systems.

7. Systematic and meaningful input by teachers, individually, in groups, and through their Association, into decisions which affect their professional practice.

8. Concentrated efforts to confront and reduce the factors that contribute to teacher stress.

9. Restoration of balance into such areas as integration and student assessment.

10. Concentrated efforts to confront and reduce the factors that contribute to teacher stress.

[1] 1. Teachers have the right to base diagnosis, planning, methodology and evaluation on professional knowledge and skills, and have the responsibility to review constantly their own level of competence and effectiveness and to seek necessary improvements as part of a continuing process of professional development.

3. [sic] Teachers have the right to a voice in all decisions of a professional nature which affect them and have the responsibility to seek the most effective means of consultation and of collaboration with their professional colleagues.

4. Teachers have the right to criticize educational programs and have the responsibility to do so in a professional manner.

Appendix 4

This slim fifty-two-page paper hails from Britain. As a government-ordered review of "available evidence about the delivery of education" in elementary grades, it presents a series of recommendations on curriculum organization, teaching methods, and classroom practice. Unlike most educational documents it is highly readable and concise. The primary author, Robin Alexander, a professor of primary education at Leeds University, has a reputation for rebuking administrators for ignoring research on what works. Not surprisingly, the document contradicts many of the practices now being advocated by educrats in Canada. The selections chosen address issues that have made the news in North America.

CURRICULUM ORGANIZATION AND CLASSROOM PRACTICE IN PRIMARY SCHOOLS: A DISCUSSION PAPER.

Robin Alexander, Professor of Primary Education, Leeds University

Jim Rose, Chief Inspector, Her Majesty's Inspectorate

Chris Woodhead, Chief Executive, National Curriculum Council

The focus of classroom research and enquiry

51 This section of the report is based on a review of the available research evidence about teaching and learning in primary schools in England, as it has accumulated over the past twenty years. The three main strands to this evidence are summarised below in order to define the context in which our discussion is set.

52 The first, and longest established, focus of enquiry is the empirical study of how primary pupils develop and learn. To teach well, teachers must take account of how children learn. We do not, however, believe that it is possible to construct a model of primary education from evidence about children's development alone: the nature of the curriculum followed by the pupil and the range of teaching strategies employed by the teacher are also of critical importance. Teaching is not applied child development. It is a weakness of the child-centred tradition that it has sometimes tended to treat it as such and, consequently, to neglect the study of classroom practice.

53 Recent research into children's learning does, however, emphasise young children's immense cognitive and linguistic competence. In the 60s and 70s, Piagetian theories about developmental ages and stages led to chronologically fixed notions of 'readiness,' thus depressing expectations and discouraging teacher intervention. More recent studies demonstrate what children, given effective teaching, can achieve and, in particular, the young child's capacity to understand the structure of subjects. They show that learning is essentially a social and interactive process. They place proper emphasis on the teacher as teacher rather than 'facilitator.' Such insights are, in our view, critical to the raising of standards in primary classrooms, and we build upon them in later sections of this report...

Curriculum structure and organisation: subjects or topics?

62 The vast majority of primary schools organise the curriculum in terms of subjects and topic work. A topic is generally understood to be a mode of curriculum organisation, frequently enquiry based, which brings elements of different subjects together under a common theme. A small minority of schools organise the whole of the curriculum in terms of separate subjects; virtually no primary school works solely

through topics. HMI report that about 30 per cent of work in primary schools is taught as single subjects. Music, physical education, most mathematics and some English are usually taught as separate subjects. The other foundation subjects are very often taught, entirely or largely, as aspects of topic work.

63 Despite these demonstrable facts, the rhetoric of primary education has for a long time been hostile to the idea that young children should be exposed to subjects. Subject divisions, it is argued, are inconsistent with the child's view of the world. Children must be allowed to construct their own meanings and subject teaching involves the imposition of a received version of knowledge. And, moreover, it is the wholeness of the curriculum which is important rather than the distinct identity of the individual subjects.

64 Each of these familiar assertions needs to be contested. First, to resist subjects on the grounds that they are inconsistent with children's views of the world is to confine them within their existing modes of thought and deny them access to some of the most powerful tools for making sense of the work which human beings have ever devised. Second, while it is self-evident that every individual, to an extent, constructs his/her own meanings, education is an encounter between these personal understandings and the public knowledge embodied in our cultural traditions. The teacher's key responsibility is to mediate such encounters so that the child's understanding is enriched. And, finally, the integrity of the curriculum as a whole is hardly likely to be achieved by sacrificing the integrity of its constituent parts....

66 We consider that a National Curriculum conceived in terms of distinct subjects makes it impossible to defend a non-differentiated curriculum. This does not mean that all the National Curriculum subjects must necessarily be taught separately: curriculum conception and modes of curriculum organisation must not be confused. But, whatever the mode of organisation, pupils must be able to grasp the particular principles and procedures of each subject, and, what is equally important, they must be able to progress from one level of knowledge, understanding and skill to another within the subject....

69 Many schools have yet, moreover, to make full use of the National Curriculum programmes of study in planning topics. Some do not

have clear, well documented schemes of work covering both key stages and detailing the subject content, knowledge and skills. Others do not provide appropriately differentiated work which caters for a full range of ability. The intrinsic complexity of topic work means that problems will remain until rigorous planning becomes the norm. Subject coherence can be lost in the attempt to subsume too much into the grand theme; key attainment targets may be given only cursory attention; monitoring and assessment can remain weak....

Mixed and single age-group classes

81 The proportion of schools with mixed age-group classes has increased from 50 to 70 per cent in the past decade. For some schools this form of grouping is a matter of choice. For most it is not, and in all schools of less than one form entry how to organise the pupils for teaching purposes is a perennial problem.

82 Teachers adopt a variety of strategies for coping in such circumstances. Some seek to individualise the tasks they set. Some use whole class teaching but try to provide open-ended activities which ostensibly allow pupils to find their own level. Some group by age, others by ability.

83 There are schools where vertical grouping has been adopted on educational grounds, but most teachers confess to finding teaching in such classes harder than in classes where pupils are relatively close in age and ability. HMI evidence suggests, too, that the considerable ability spread inevitable in the mixed age class leads to poor match of task to pupil in a third of the classes and a general failure to challenge the most able pupils. Planning, monitoring and assessment are particularly demanding in these circumstances. These constraints must, we believe, be acknowledged as a factor to be considered whenever the viability of small schools is discussed....

Individual teaching

88 Given the self-evident fact that every child is different, individual teaching is an understandable aspiration. Indeed there are times when individual pupils will need particular help from one teacher. Pupils, for example, with learning difficulties will need one-to-one teaching for some of the time. However, it must be said that children have

much in common, and that, in practice, the effort to teach every pupil in the class as an individual is fraught with difficulties. In such circumstances, the evidence shows that however skilled and energetic the teacher, each individual pupil receives a minute proportion of the teacher's attention. The interaction between teacher and pupil is likely to be as superficial as it is brief and infrequent. Pupils, deprived of the attention from either the teacher or other pupils which will maintain their motivation and challenge their thinking, work only intermittently. Not surprisingly, research studies show relatively low gains in pupil understanding in classrooms where teachers structure the day largely in terms of individual teaching. Teachers should not be tempted by approaches to teaching, which, when taken to extremes, can result in low level individual tasks and fleeting and superficial teacher/pupil interaction.

Whole class teaching

89 Whole class teaching appears to provide the order, control, purpose and concentration which many critics believe are lacking in modern primary classrooms.

90 To a significant extent, the evidence supports this view of whole class teaching. Whole class teaching is associated with higher-order questioning, explanations and statements, and these in turn correlate with higher levels of pupil performance. Teachers with a substantial commitment to whole class teaching appear, moreover, to be particularly effective in teaching the basic subjects.

91 The potential weaknesses of whole class teaching need, however, to be acknowledged. There is a tendency for the teaching to be pitched too much towards the middle of the ability range, and thus to risk losing the less able and boring the brightest. Observational studies show that pupils pay attention and remain on task when being taught as a class, but may, in fact, slow down their rate of working to meet the teacher's norm, thus narrowing the challenge of what is taught to an extent which advocates of whole class teaching might well find uncomfortable.

92 Despite these potential weaknesses whole class teaching is an essential teaching skill, which all primary school teachers should be able to deploy as appropriate. Provided that the teacher has a firm grasp of

the subject matter to be taught and the skills to involve the class, pupils' thinking can be advanced very effectively.

Matching the task to the pupil

107 Standards of education in primary schools will not rise until teachers expect more of their pupils, and, in particular, more of able and disadvantaged children.

108 The problem is partly ideological. In some schools and local education authorities the legitimate drive to create equal opportunities for all pupils has resulted in an obsessive fear of anything which, in the jargon, might be deemed 'elitist'. As a consequence, the needs of some of our most able children have quite simply not been met. There has also been a tendency to stereotype, and, in particular, to assume that social disadvantage leads inevitably to educational failure. This waste of potential must not continue....

Assessing and recording progress

111 HMI surveys since the 70s show that pupil assessment has often been a largely intuitive process. Records have been similarly idiosyncratic and have tended to be limited to the basics and to focus on tasks encountered rather than learning achieved. Until recently, parents often received generalised, laconic statements which offered little real insight into the progress their children had made....

116 Assessment and record-keeping are not synonymous, though they are frequently treated as such. There is little point in developing an elaborate record-keeping system if the evidence upon which the records are based is inadequate. The pre-condition for good records is, therefore, good assessment. Indeed, there is some evidence that record keeping may become an end in itself: cumbersome, time consuming and of little value to either teacher or pupil. The purposes and recipients of records need to be clearly identified and the records constructed accordingly.

Conclusion: key issues in classroom practice

117 We wish, first, to acknowledge the professional commitment and skill shown by primary teachers over the last two years. It is primary teachers

in general (and Year 1 and 2 teachers in particular) who have faced the most daunting challenge in implementing the National Curriculum. We have no doubt whatsoever that very significant progress has been made.

118 We believe, however, that a new professional climate is needed. In recent decades much teaching in primary schools has suffered from highly questionable dogmas which have generated excessively complex classroom practice and have devalued the role of subjects in the curriculum. The new climate must encourage teachers to review their teaching techniques in the light of evidence about effective classroom practice and how well the pupils are making progress....

126 Standards will not rise until teachers demand more of their pupils. Over-complex patterns of classroom organisation frustrate assessment, diagnosis and task matching, and preoccupy teachers with management matters rather than learning tasks....

128 The achievement of progress in learning is the touchstone for all decisions about teaching. Good teaching does not merely keep step with the pupils but challenges and stretches their thinking.

Appendix 5

TEN RECOMMENDED BOOKS ON EDUCATION

Marilyn Jager Adams. *Beginning to Read: Thinking and Learning about Print: A Summary*. Center for the Study of Reading, The Reading Research and Education Center, University of Illinois at Urbana-Champaign, 1990. The best report yet written on the reading debate.

Jacques Barzun. *Begin Here: The Forgotten Conditions of Teaching and Learning*. Chicago: University of Chicago Press, 1991. A collection of fifteen excellent essays by an American educator rich in common sense. A classic book on teaching and learning.

Allan Bloom. *The Closing of the American Mind*. New York: Simon and Schuster, 1987. The first half of the book is a brilliant critique of technological society; the second half loses its way.

R.G. Des Dixon. *Future Schools and How to Get There From Here: A Primer for Evolutionaries*. Toronto: ECW Press, 1992. A radical perspective on school reform that is equally full of brilliant insights and technocratic illusions.

Jacques Ellul. *The Humiliation of the Word*. Grand Rapids, Michigan: William B. Eerdmans Publishing Company, 1985. A dense but brilliant analysis of how computers, television, and other audio-visual tools have diminished the word and the teaching of the word by one of the world's most foremost Christian philosophers.

Northrop Frye. *On Education*. Toronto: Fitzhenry and Whiteside, 1990. Solid and reliable reading on good teaching.

William K. Kilpatrick. *Why Johnny Can't Tell Right From Wrong*. Toronto: Simon and Schuster, 1992. A rigorous exposé of how "values clarification" or moral reasoning is neither a sane nor particularly moral replacement for good old-fashioned character development.

Hilda Neatby. *A Temperate Dispute*. Toronto: Clarke, Irwin and Company Limited, 1954. A prophetic work on schooling and a companion piece to So Little For the Mind by a long-forgotten feminist and nationalist.

Neil Postman. *Technology: The Surrender of Culture to Technology*. New York: Alfred A. Knopf, 1992. A lucid critique of technology and its impact on education.

Harold W. Stevenson and James W. Stigler. *The Learning Gap: Why Our Schools Are Failing and What We Can Learn From Japanese and Chinese Education*. Toronto: Summit Books, 1992. As the authors carefully detail, the only lessons we can really learn are ones that we have abandoned or forgotten.

Appendix 6

Several years ago Jerry Mander, a television critic and former advertising executive, wrote *In the Absence of the Sacred*, a thoughtful but not entirely coherent book about technology and Indians. It does contain, however, one insightful passage on how to keep a human perspective in a society inundated with propaganda about the benefits of technology. Every school could review these guidelines before buying computer or any other "gee-whiz" equipment.

TEN RECOMMENDED ATTITUDES ABOUT TECHNOLOGY

Now we are about to move into a new technological age, the brave new world of space colonies, laser weapons and communications, genetic engineering, robotics, and so on. We are already hearing familiar-sounding claims that this new generation of technologies will finally deliver that brighter, more glorious future. Part II of this book will present detailed analyses of some of these new technologies as well as some of the ones that are already upon us. Meanwhile, I offer here a little list of reminders that I keep printed above my own desk. They help me maintain appropriate attitudes to protect against the one-sided information onslaught. Perhaps they'll be useful to you.

I. Since most of what we are told about new technology comes from its proponents, be deeply skeptical of all claims.

2. Assume all technology "guilty until proven innocent."

3. Eschew the idea that technology is neutral or "value free." Every technology has *inherent and identifiable* social, political, and environmental consequences.

4. The fact that technology has a natural flash and appeal is meaningless. Negative attributes are slow to emerge.

5. Never judge a technology by the way it benefits you personally. Seek a holistic view of its impacts. The operative question is not whether it benefits you, but who benefits most? And to what end?

6. Keep in mind that an individual technology is only one piece of a larger web of technologies, "megatechnology." The operative question here is how the individual technology fits the larger one.

7. Make distinctions between technologies that primarily serve the individual or the small community (e.g., solar energy) and those that operate on a scale outside of community control (e.g., nuclear energy). The latter kind is the problem of the day.

8. When it is argued that the benefits of the technological lifeway are worthwhile despite harmful outcomes, recall that Lewis Mumford referred to these alleged benefits as "bribery." Cite the figures about crime, suicide, alienation, drug abuse, as well as environmental and cultural degradation.

9. Do not accept the homily that "once the genie is out of the bottle you cannot put it back," or that rejecting a technology is impossible. Such attitudes induce passivity and confirm victimization.

10. In thinking about technology within the present climate of technological worship, emphasize the negative. This brings balance. Negativity is positive.

Appendix 7

INTERNATIONAL TEST SCORES

Although international test scores often compare apples with oranges, they do reflect general learning and teaching trends. In this regard they show that Canada's school system is not teaching its pupils as well as its administrators pretend it is. The following tables, assembled by the Organization for Quality Education (OQE), indicate that Ontario's French Immersion schools either don't do a lot of math or science teaching or don't do it very well.

Mathematics Test Results
1991 International Assessment of Educational Progress II (IAEP II)

Results for students 13 years old—Gr.8 by Country

	Average % correct
Korea	73
Taiwan	73
Switzerland	71
CIS (USSR)	70
Hungary	68
France	64
Emilia-Romagna, Italy	64
Israel (Hebrew schools)	63
Canada	62
Scotland	61
Ireland	61
Slovenia	57
Spain	55
United States	55
Jordan	40

Results for students 13 years old—Gr.8 by Province

	Average % correct
Quebec French	69
Saskatchewan French	68
BC	66
Quebec English	66
Alberta	64
Manitoba French	63
Saskatchewan English	62
New Brunswick French	61
Nova Scotia	60
Newfoundland	59
Manitoba English	58
New Brunswick English	58
Ontario English	58
Ontario French	53

Most of the questions for this test were from Ontario Gr.4 and Gr.5 textbooks, that is for students 9 and 10 years old. Earlier results showed that while Korea was marginally ahead of Ontario on simple questions, Korean students were *five times better* than Ontario students with the hardest level questions.

Science Test Results
1991 International Assessment of Educational Progress II (IAEP II)

Results for students 13 years old—Gr.8 by Country

	Average % correct
Korea	78
Taiwan	76
Switzerland	74
Hungary	73
CIS (USSR)	71
Slovenia	70
Emilia-Romagna, Italy	70
Israel (Hebrew schools)	70
Canada	69
France	69
Scotland	68
Spain	68
United States	67
Ireland	63
Jordan	57

Results for students 13 years old—Gr.8
by Province

	Average % correct
Alberta	74
BC	72
Quebec French	71
Saskatchewan English	70
Quebec English	69
Nova Scotia	69
Manitoba English	69
Manitoba French	67
Ontario English	67
New Brunswick English	66
Newfoundland	66
Saskatchewan French	65
New Brunswick French	64
Ontario French	53

Appendix 8

In 1987 George Radwanski completed a review of Ontario's system of education: "Ontario's Study of the Relevance of Education and the Issue of Dropouts." Although championed by ordinary people, educators ignored the report. In New Brunswick, however, the government recently adopted many of its sensible recommendations. Radwanski's recipe for school improvement still makes cogent reading and has unwittingly defined many of the goals of the nation's school reform movement.

BEGINNING TO READ: THINKING AND LEARNING ABOUT PRINT

Summary of Recommendations (Radwanski Report)

1. That the emphasis of educational philosophy in Ontario be shifted from process to outcomes, and that the objectives of education be defined in terms of the acquisition of specified demonstrable knowledge and skills by all children, through the application of pedagogical techniques appropriate to each child's needs.

2. That the essential content of education in Ontario for all students be defined in terms of the acquisition of demonstrable knowledge and/or skills in the following areas: English (reading,

writing, speaking and listening); clear thinking and effective learning; mathematics; literature; the sciences and technology; Canadian and world history; Canadian and world geography; citizenship; work in society; French; the arts; and fitness and health.

3. That the Ministry of Education specifically prescribe program content and the necessary knowledge/skills outcomes on a province-wide basis, while delegating to local authorities the selection of pedagogical techniques for teaching that content and bringing about the prescribed outcomes for all students.

4. That it be made an explicit and vigorously pursued goal of education policy in Ontario to have all students, except those precluded by severe mental or physical disability, continue in high school until graduation.

5. That high-quality educational outcomes for all students and retention of all students in high school until graduation be seen as necessarily parallel and complementary, not competing, objectives and that they be vigorously pursued simultaneously.

6. That the Ministry of Education proceed with any specific dropout prevention initiatives only on the understanding that they are a stop-gap measure to be undertaken strictly in conjunction with, and not as a substitute for, urgent progress in addressing fundamental issues in our elementary and secondary systems of education.

7. That the Ministry of Education conduct a major and sustained advertising campaign, using television and other media including posters in the schools, to emphasize to students and their parents the importance of remaining in high school until graduation.

8. That, in addition, all school boards be required to conduct advertising and communications campaigns urging parents to encourage their children to stay in high school until graduation and to contact the school if their children are contemplating dropping out or are experiencing other problems.

9. That all high schools in Ontario be required to assign every student to a teacher who will be responsible for monitoring that student's progress in all courses, for promptly identifying

any signs of academic or personal difficulties, and for initiating interventions as appropriate to assist the student with any such difficulties.

10. That all high schools be required to provide regular weekly individual mentoring sessions with teachers at the very least for students whose background or academic characteristics indicate a risk of dropping out, and that mentoring also be provided to other students to the maximum extent made possible by recourse as necessary to qualified mentors from the community at large.

11. That all high schools be required to provide high-quality remediation and tutoring services for students who are experiencing academic difficulties.

12. That consideration be given to contracting with community-based social service agencies to locate teams of appropriate professionals within high schools to provide troubled young people with ready access to services such as crisis intervention, family counselling, economic and social counselling, and help with psychological, emotional or medical problems.

13. That every school board be required to provide infant-care and child-care facilities for students in at least one of its high schools or—in areas where the need is insufficient to justify in-school facilities—to provide students with fully subsidized and accessible infant-care or child-care arrangements outside the school.

14. That all high schools be required to make contact, normally through the monitoring or mentoring teacher, with all students who drop out during the school year or who fail to return in the fall, in order to establish the reasons for their decision, to make a genuine effort to persuade them to reconsider and, if that fails, to explain the opportunities for return at a later date.

15. That all school boards in Ontario be required to provide universally available early childhood education in public and separate schools for children from the age of 3.

16. That the Government of Ontario provide appropriate financial assistance to the school boards for the provision of such early childhood education.

17. That the availability and importance of early childhood education be vigorously publicized to parents, with special efforts devoted to encouraging parents in the lowest socio-economic status groups to take advantage of this opportunity for their children.

18. That policies and practices in Ontario's elementary schools be founded on the premise that all children, except those with specific and insuperable mental or physical handicaps, can be brought to a common necessary level of knowledge and skills through the application of appropriate pedagogical techniques.

19. That the practice of homogeneous ability grouping for instruction in any subject be discontinued by all schools in Ontario and, if necessary to achieve this result, that it be expressly prohibited by the Ministry of Education.

20. That the spiral curriculum approach be abandoned as an educational practice in Ontario elementary schools.

21. That in place of the spiral curriculum, educational policy in Ontario set clear and sequential outcome goals for each grade.

22. That within each elementary school grade the essential principles of the mastery learning approach be incorporated at least to the extent of treating learning tasks in each subject area as sequential, having students successfully master each task before moving on to the next, and providing students with whatever individualized help they may need to cope successfully with each such task.

23. That standardized province-wide tests at least in reading comprehension, writing (including grammar, spelling and punctuation), mathematics, reasoning and problem-solving, and learning skills, as well as in other core curriculum subjects in high school, be administered to all elementary and high school students at appropriate intervals throughout the years of schooling.

24. That such standardized province-wide testing be primarily diagnostic in purpose, leading to appropriate remedial initiatives for all students whose performance on the tests indicate difficulties in one or more areas.

25. That automatic social promotion of children who are significantly behind grade level in learning accomplishment be

replaced by enrollment in summer remediation programs, followed by evaluation as to whether sufficient progress has been made to enable them to keep up with the work of the next grade, with or without further remedial help during the school year.

26. That, as a necessary last resort, children who have not progressed sufficiently in summer remediation to be able to keep up with the work of the next grade be retained for a year for further remediation, preferably in a special remedial group with greater opportunity for individualized attention than in regular classes.

27. That the current policy of streaming high school students into academic, general and basic courses of study be abolished, and replaced by provision of a single and undifferentiated high-quality educational stream for all students.

28. That the credit system be abolished or phased out and replaced with a common program of learning in the essential content areas for all; students, with no optional courses in Grades 9 and 10, and with only a limited number of optional courses to the degree consistent with successful learning outcomes in the essential content areas in Grades 11 and 12.

29. That students remain together in a stable heterogeneous class grouping for most of their common subjects each year, and that, if possible, the class teacher provide instruction in a minimum of two subjects to provide sustained teacher-student contact.

30. That increasing use be made of computers for remedial instruction in the elementary and secondary schools, but only with the clear understanding that computers are not a substitute for—and should only be used in conjunction with—personalized and sustained remedial attention by a teacher.

31. That high schools take a pro-active role in making all students aware of the damage that excessive part-time work can do to their educational prospects, and that consideration be given to specifying in school codes of conduct the acceptable maximums of part-time work during the school year.

32. That high schools and/or boards of education explore the feasibility and desirability of cooperative programs with the

business community to provide students who wish it with limited amounts of part-time work contingent on maintaining
satisfactory marks and school attendance.

33. That the business community, and individual businesses of
every size, recognize the short-sightedness and social irresponsibility of providing students with excessive part-time work
during the school year or encouraging students to leave school
for full-time employment.

34. That the full-range of extra-curricular activities continue to be
recognized as a vital element of the program rather than a frill
in all high schools, and that high schools make an active effort
to encourage the participation of all students in such activities.

35. That the legal school leaving age not be modified at this time,
but that all participants in the system of education at every
level be regarded as accountable for doing everything possible
to motivate, encourage and assist all young people to continue
in high school, until graduation.

Appendix 9

This powerful letter, written by an Ontario high school history teacher, eloquently makes a plea for a return to teaching and learning in our schools. The author's name cannot be revealed: his school board does not value public discourses.

LETTER FROM A TEACHER

This spring, for the first time in my career, I was a participant in a six week teachers' strike. I was enormously surprised to find myself doing picket duty. I never thought I would ever be called on to do such a thing. Now that the strike is over and only the nasty echoes remain, I can finally see some benefits emerging from what I and my colleagues collectively endured. The strike has shown me that I should have spoken out years ago and offered up my classroom experience as a practical, useful measure for what needs to be done to improve public education. That I didn't do so is now a source of considerable regret to me. Perhaps if I, and hundreds like me, had quietly insisted we be heard, things might have been different this spring. But then again, maybe I'm hopelessly naive.

The labour dispute in which I played a supporting—and very minor—role did not emerge overnight. Disagreement over money may have been the catalyst that stimulated the strike, but it was for me, and so many others, disappointment with the educational choices we have made over the past ten or fifteen years that was the real source of dissatisfaction. In education, we are prisoners of the good idea. Our problem is not that we do too little, but rather, that we try to do too much.

Who can say at what point one more good idea becomes too much? Because our attention tends to focus on the individual merits of each new idea as it is presented, it is easy for us to lose sight of the final burden that has to be borne by the system to sustain each new initiative. Finally though, as more and more is piled on, the burden imposed by all we are asked to do becomes too great and the quality of education suffers.

I have a thousand excuses for having remained silent. However, when I look back on these excuses after six weeks of walking in the snow and rain, they all seem so self-serving. I can still hear myself enumerating my reasons for keeping quiet: I'm just the hired help; I don't make policy; I'm not sitting on top of the mountain and therefore I can't see "the big picture"; those in charge surely must know what is best. But by far the most important reason for my silence is even simpler than any of these, admittedly, unsatisfactory reasons: *no one ever asked me.* Not once in the past quarter century did anyone ever seek me out to ask my opinion on how best to spend the available tax dollars. To be sure, from time to time, I did receive surveys—questionnaires—that gave the impression I was being consulted but they were always so general as to elicit nothing very useful. Real decisions are made when money is allocated. Invariably, my involvement began after the allocation had been decided. Now I realize I should have come forward on my own and spoken up—not to try and take on a role that is not rightly mine—but instead to offer the help of my experience. I don't think anyone would see my speaking out as impertinent. After all, I know my place. I'm still just a spear carrier in this great educational army. Yet, the spear carriers are the ones who must first endure the tactical mistakes the generals make. Somewhat surprisingly, I've found that this same experience also helps them to pick out many of the strategic errors as well.

During the strike, I didn't like the way we were portrayed by almost all the media. Repeatedly we were depicted as greedy, overpaid, underworked public employees whose demands were at the heart of what is wrong with public education. The solutions that emerged over and over again from this view were depressingly similar: curb the teachers' excessive wage demands, make them work harder, impose centralized testing to hold them accountable and all will be well in our public schools. Rather than being part of the solution, we were shown as *the* central problem.

Certainly, that's not a picture I recognize of myself or my colleagues. I work with a very bright, highly talented group of people. We are not dumb driven sheep. We have ideas and we very much want to do a good job. We should be heard. If the discussions I have been involved in with my colleagues in the privacy of our staffrooms and offices is any accurate indicator, I can assure you, we *can* propose ways not only to spend scarce tax dollars wisely but also to improve and enhance the skills of the students we teach. Educational policy is not set in a vacuum. It is worked out in reaction to the prevailing ideas that regularly cross the public stage. Ours is a vigorous educational democracy in which many voices are raised, usually in criticism of some real or perceived shortcoming of our schools. That is, I think, as it should be. Public comments must always be encouraged. The problem I see with this process is the unwillingness—deliberate or otherwise—to involve the *classroom* teacher in the assessment of the many changes discussed and introduced. We hear so much these days that Canada's economic future depends on a highly skilled work force collaborating as part of a management/labour team to make and keep the nation competitive. Top down management, I have found, is more the norm, with meaningful consultation, the exception.

Although I have taught for over twenty-five years, most of my time has been spent in just one school. Some would, undoubtedly, see my twenty-two-year period in the same school as an oddity and a handicap. I, however, see it as a distinct advantage when it comes to measuring the value of the many changes that have come to education over the years. Being in one place for an extended time has given me the luxury of being able to filter out the background noise that frequently, I think, obscures the vision of my more mobile colleagues. I believe they find it harder to measure the impact of change when they move to new communities they don't know as well as I know this one. I have to take many fewer variables into account when I assess the value of each change I've faced. In such a controlled environment, my personal observations, I believe, made keen by years of detailed practice, cannot be fooled easily or readily dismissed. I don't mean to sound pompous by speaking this way. I'm not trying to set myself up as a repository of revealed wisdom. I know that objections will immediately be raised against this assertion. One such objection will be that teachers are more than adequately represented by the many professional groups that regularly appear before the Trustees and the Ministry of Education. Although I could challenge this assertion in great detail, that would take me down another road that I don't want to explore at the moment. Suffice it to say, there are many organizations that speak *for* me; there are far fewer that speak *with* me.

With these introductory observations aside, I thought it might be helpful if I presented some examples in education where I would very much like to be given the opportunity to share some insights gained through practical, first-hand experience. In no sense is this a complete list. To do that, I'd have to write the book everyone claims they want to write. Consider these few examples to be simple illustrations of the broader points I'm trying to make. (In doing so, I'll not make any references that are uniquely local in nature. I've already told you I'm a powerless classroom teacher—a spear carrier in the great army. Although that role has many disadvantages, it is, I think, far better than raising issues that might get me re-assigned as a spear catcher.)

Let's start, by looking at computers in education for no particular reason other than it's a trendy topic that neatly illustrates the difficulties created by the good idea. That the community considers the introduction of this technology into education to be a good idea is impossible to challenge. After all, who could be opposed to equipping our young people with the technical skills they need to function in the twenty-first century? Certainly not me if I thought that's what we were, in fact, doing.

Millions of dollars have been spent on computers in education to achieve, in my opinion, very little. I do not attach any blame to the educational community for this failure. It has simply responded to the silly—but very powerful notion—that the quality of education in the classroom varies in direct proportion to the number of computers available in the school. The popular perception is that the more computers there are in a school, the better the education provided by that school.

Early in the 1980's, computers began to make their way in considerable numbers into our schools. From the outset I have willingly worked and experimented with these machines. I am no Luddite. In doing so, I have found them to be of great value in supporting my work in the classroom. Therefore, I would be delighted to see these machines play an educationally useful classroom role as well. Unfortunately, after over a decade of trying, I have personally achieved very indifferent results and, search as I might for examples of *realistic* classroom success, I have encountered previous few. I would caution anyone who raises as rebuttal, the many computer demonstrations that are routinely presented to show the wonderful things these machines can accomplish in the classroom. Be very suspicious. I have witnessed many of these demonstrations. Who among us has not, at one time or another, watched and subsequently succumbed to a demonstration of some wonderful gadget by purchasing it—vegetable choppers spring to mind—only to find it either impossible to reproduce the demonstrated results at home or to find out it demanded so much time and effort to so do that it was faster and easier to complete the job in some other way. If you don't believe me, I suggest you count the number of unused—or underused—machines stored away in the kitchen cupboards of the nation. That is the dilemma, I believe, facing teachers who are willing to try to integrate these machines into the classroom. Sadly, far more is promised than the current technology is capable of delivering. I wouldn't be very concerned about this shortcoming if we were just being asked to continue experimenting with this technology. After all, it's through constant experimentation that innovation is best assessed to determine if it is truly useful. Unfortunately, with this technology still unproved, we are about to embark on a full scale implementation drive to "encourage" much greater classroom use of computers. Weekly time quotas will be set for student computer usage. No doubt, at the same time, teachers will be monitored to ensure compliance with this new educational goal. By doing so, teachers are, again, I would argue, being set up as scapegoats for any implementation problems that result.

Whenever I have spoken with my colleagues—or anyone else for that matter—about the technical limitations of the equipment we have been given, there is usually more agreement than disagreement. Yet, surprisingly, in almost the same instant, someone always puts forth the same justification for pushing ahead with implementation anyway. We must ensure, so this argument goes, the development of better equipment and software for our use tomorrow, by providing today, the incentive of a healthy market to the producers of these goods.

In addition to the technical shortcomings I have attempted to describe, there are two additionally powerful reasons for being concerned about the direction we are heading with computers. Teachers are being asked to devote enormous amounts of teaching and preparation time to this equipment to help students acquire, what, I believe, are, more often than not, very low level skills ("Turn on the machine, insert the disc, make a selection from the menu") while, at the same time, watching scarce education dollars being spent in the process. We have a finite amount of time with which to work. If we try to squeeze more into the available time, something else has to be abandoned or else suffer from neglect.

Many will object that I am being too hard on this emerging technology. They will point to wonderful examples of computers being successfully used to integrate higher level thinking skills into the learning process. I too have witnessed such examples. However, over the years, I have learned to adopt a healthy skepticism when presented with results that seem too good to be true. They usually are.

There are students in every school who would turn up at midnight during a blinding blizzard for a class held on the school's football field for the chance to work with these machines. Their work is truly amazing. They and their supporters are passionate proselytizers working to fulfil the promise of this technology. Too often though, their work is held up as the norm instead of the exception I believe it to be.

What's the rush? Why can't we wait for performance to catch up with promise? Education holds a very special position in our society. It is one of the bed rock institutions that binds our society together. Proceeding with reform too quickly is done at our collective peril. Unfortunately, we tend to get stampeded by our fears. We're afraid that we're falling behind (whatever that means) in the great global race for educational excellence. Added to that fear is the North American tendency to seek a technological cure for almost every problem.

Rapid technological obsolescence and the need for perpetual care are the twin sources of much of this ongoing financial burden. These machines can be very temperamental. Heaven knows they have to ensure "enthusiastic" student use. In the board of education I work for, there are employees whose job it is to anticipate such problems and to care for this equipment so that it will be ready when needed.

In 1969, the Ontario government completed a massive reorganization of the school boards in this province. The school board I work for was created as a result of this reorganization. When it began operation, it inherited responsibility for about 19,000 students. Its head office started out with 22 employees. Now, twenty-two years later, there are about 42,000 students in attendance in this board's schools and, the last time I counted the names in the head office telephone directory, there were more than 400 people listed there. Put another way, while the student population has slightly more than doubled, the support staff has increased nearly twentyfold. Please note, I'm not, in any way, suggesting these people are not hard working, dedicated individuals. I'm just trying to use this one example to show that the cost of education has steadily gone up over the years because new programs have regularly been added and new responsibilities mandated with the result that great expense has been incurred. Remember, none of these support people I've mentioned directly teaches students.

Now contrast what I have just described with this situation.

During this same twenty-two-year period, I have been teaching in the same classroom in the same school. Over all that time, while the support staff has been steadily increasing, my classroom has been painted just once. The original carpet is still on the floor and all the desks and chairs are the same as the day the school opened.

My point?

The costs of change are clear to me, the benefits far less so.

So far, in discussing computers in education, I've really only touched on financial and time costs even though there are other more significant costs to be noted. To get a handle on these other costs, it's necessary to re-visit the great debate of "process versus content" which still rages in education. The process camp—and that usually includes those who advocate more computer usage in our schools—repeat an educational philosophy that has practically become a religious incantation to its supporters. It goes something like this: Knowledge is expanding exponentially. Therefore, it is more important to teach students how to learn than it is to teach them a specific body of discrete facts that will become outdated even before it can be committed to memory.

Overcoming the damage done by this philosophy is, I believe, the single greatest challenge we have to face in education today.

I have several reasons for saying so.

First, I don't believe that the rapidly expanding rate of knowledge has eliminated the need for a rigorous, broadly based, compulsory education in basic principles. In fact, it is precisely because our knowledge in all spheres is increasing so quickly that students, more than ever before, need a basic education in which their course selections are very largely made for them.

By doing so, we can at least be reasonably certain that they have been exposed to a wide range of educational experiences. At a minimum, let's make them look at the various forests growing around them so that even though the trees, over the years, multiply in number, they'll still know what they're looking at.

Let me use what has happened to geography courses in our secondary schools as an example of why I think a more directive approach to student course selection is needed. Very few students study this subject any more. We could spend a long time discussing whether or not there is a place in the compulsory curriculum for such a subject. I don't teach geography but it would be a prime candidate for greater exposure in any curriculum I would design. My reason for selecting this subject—and all the other curricular areas important to me—is that this subject gives students essential information I feel they need to become minimally literate. Rather than put forth my case for all the specific course selections I would make, let me just say that our current approach favours non-intervention or more precisely, selective non-intervention. I'm not as concerned about the specific choices as I am about our unwillingness to be more direct with students. Unfortunately, what we usually say is let the market decide. The result has been very sad and all too predictable. To the process school, declining enrolment in this area is no cause for alarm. Students equipped with the skills of information retrieval will be able to tap into the data banks of the world to capture any geographical information they may someday need. And yet, I wonder. Just because a student knows how to retrieve something doesn't mean he will know what to retrieve. *If you don't know that you don't know...then what?* In such a situation, how do you frame appropriate questions so that your precious process education skills can rescue you from the prison of your ignorance? I know lots of students who are in this very situation. Their education has done them a terrible disservice. They don't even know how ignorant they are.

I hope my point is clear. When process education alters the traditional curriculum, it maintains that this change better equips students for the world in which they will live. The burden of proof though lies with those who advocate this approach. So far, I have heard nothing from them that is reassuring. I believe that a broadly based liberal education is still the best preparation for the world in which our students will be living when they graduate. The problems created by our unwillingness to teach and assess students more rigorously will continue to show up in many different ways. Please tell me, because I really want to know, the answer to the following question: If our young people don't know they don't know what it means to be a Canadian, a westerner, a world citizen, how can you expect them to treasure and protect their inheritance? To be ignorant of the history, the geography, the literature, the scientific tradition that have shaped western society is both a personal and a national tragedy. To leave much educational selection up to the changing tastes—dare I say whims?—of the individual raises a question not yet satisfactorily answered: Who speaks for collective interests? How long, I ask, can a liberal democracy effectively function if its citizenry can't articulate, let alone understand the shared values that have shaped their culture?

Before I finish, let me present one more piece of evidence to try to fix my point clearly. In the school in which I teach, every January students are asked to make their course selections for the following year. They are given about a month to consider their choices. As the time for option sheet submission draws near, students are repeatedly reminded of how important these selections are. Homeform teachers are directed to encourage students to submit their option sheets by the advertised date. Announcements, both written and oral, are sent out by the school's administration to ensure compliance. Guidance counsellors stand ready to advise students on the wisdom of what they propose to do. After all of this effort to get the job done, on the day selected for form submission, *fully two-thirds* of the students fail to hand in their forms on time. This is a pattern that has repeated itself for many years now. To get the forms completed, a special compulsory assembly is mandated which all students who have not handed in their forms are required to attend. Here they sit until they have finally chosen their courses for next year. I believe it is a truism that people always have time to do what they want to do and never enough time to do everything else. With that thought in mind, I have this nagging suspicion that students do not take course selection all that seriously. Is this haphazard student approach to their future, the promise of process education? To me there is a better alternative. What I am arguing for is what we have traditionally done—admittedly imperfectly—in our schools. We still have a need for a broadly based liberal education that *rigorously* insists that students acquire— and prove that they have acquired—a wide variety of necessary skills and knowledge. I believe it is our responsibility to be much more prescriptive in students' educational lives. We're doing both them and ourselves a disservice by not intervening firmly and making our expectations clear.

Who knows? If we change our approach, student homework might actually get done on occasion.

I've just barely begun to talk about the issues that concern me. However, I've probably written enough that, by now, you'll be able to get some idea of how I assess the educational world around me. I would like to do something to help improve education; being controversial, for its own sake, holds no appeal for me at all.

Appendix 10

PROGRESSIVE VERSUS POPULIST SCHOOLING

Most of the conflicts in education originate with two conflicting ideas about schooling. In one camp, educators hail progressive child-centred methods that academics call "constructivism"; in the other, parents and teachers champion traditional notions of schooling that are community-minded and populist in orientation. The following chart, adapted from several sources, spells out the radical differences.

Progressive

1. Knowledge cannot be transferred, it must be invented by the learner. Knowledge grows out of solving problems in meaningful, natural contexts.
2. Meaningful learning is accomplished by allowing students to develop, invent, or construct their own strategies and concepts.
3. Independent problem solving is the root of learning.

Populist

1. Knowledge is transferrable. It is what one generation passes to the next. Knowledge is most efficiently transferred by systematic instruction.
2. Meaning is taught by presenting carefully sequenced strategies that require constant mindful discrimination.
3. Independent problem solving is the application of learning.

4. Motivation springs from the child; the classroom environment can only provide support.
5. Learning takes place in collaborative groups where pupils set the pace, make presentations, and take charge of their own learning.

4. The teacher can inspire and motivate children with effective instructional tools and clear testing.
5. Learning takes place in groups, some collaborative, some not, but where the teacher or the curriculum sets the pace and structures learning for the most effective and reliable results.

Notes

CHAPTER ONE:

1. The level of violence in Canadian schools is routinely covered up by image-conscious school boards. In an unusual display of honesty, the Calgary Board of Education recently published the results of a high school survey that found that one in five students carried "some sort of weapon" to class because they didn't feel safe in school. Whether reported or not, gang fights, sexual assault, and vandalism to washrooms, school buses, and parked cars are now routine occurrences in most large Canadian schools. In many of North America's major cities, policemen routinely patrol school buildings. South of the border, an estimated 525,000 attacks, robberies, rapes, and other crimes occur in public schools every month.

    Dan Wiseman, chief of Social Services for the Ottawa Board of Education, noted in a recent issue of *Orbit*, "We have a stereotype of who these young people are. They're not street kids, the traditional view, or the West Side story gangs, the Americanized view. They tend to be kids in school, using school as an area of association, being violent in school, to school, from school, at shopping centres, on bus routes, and we've seen a whole growth of extremely pervasive and destructive behaviour that contaminates, with very few participants, an entire school."

2. Ruth Weir, an Etobicoke teacher, documents these facts in "Philosophy, Cultural Beliefs and Literacy," *Interchange*, Vol. 21 (Winter, 1990), 24-33. At the turn of the century, Canada, like Scandinavia,

had one of the highest literacy rates in the world. According to a 1931 census, the government reported an illiteracy rate (an inability to read or write) of only 3.73 per cent. Canada has progressed, however, and followed the American example: its illiteracy rate, depending on the rigour of the definition, hovers between 20 and 30 per cent.

CHAPTER TWO

I. As an educational vehicle, the frightful inadequacy of activity centres became clear in a 1978 study by the Etobicoke Board of Education in Metropolitan Toronto. Originally designed by Mary Ann Evans and Brian Usher to show the superiority of play, the study compared the performance of ten child-centred, play-based projects from Grades I to 3 with ten "traditional," teacher-directed classrooms.

To the dismay of play's disciples, the study found that formal classrooms fostered achievement in reading and mathematics "to a greater extent" than the experimental classes where some teachers "did not yet get around to teaching reading."

It also concluded that sandboxes, water tables, and fantasy props could be beneficial, but to make a difference, they required structured interventions and direction from highly skilled teachers, "which was not the case in the classrooms observed....When children played, the teacher was seldom involved."

Although the top performers in both programs differed little in achievement (indicating that parents might have made the difference or that top performers learn no matter what you throw at them), the lower performers tell a very different story.

Here the results showed that the average academic performance of the play kids began at the level where the lowest performers in the traditional program stopped, which means that a steady diet of play simply made the poor children academically poorer and conditioned them for a life of poverty.

2. Lawr and Gidney, pp. 213-215.

3. Toch, pp. 48-50.

4. Unlike many other parts of the world, North America has classes for the slow, the gifted, the learning disabled, the inattentive, and the ill-

behaved. And like most educational institutions, these special education classes have grown so much that many Canadian school boards now identify more than a quarter of their children as participants in or candidates for "special education."

All of this well-intended specialness has far too often streamed or slotted working-class children into dead-end classes. Studies done in England and by the Toronto Board of Education show that students directed towards special classes (other than those for the deaf and blind) come mainly from blue-collar or immigrant families. As noted in *Stacking the Deck*, a book examining this practice, the evidence paints a portrait of a system that "segregates many students from their peers, often for long periods of time, in low expectation 'behavioural' programs on the basis of subjective reporting and culturally biased testing."

In contrast to this academic child abuse, European and Asian educators take a different stand. Europeans acknowledge that a small percentage of children (perhaps 5 per cent) will be hard to teach because of genuine learning disabilities, but Asians don't believe that individual differences among children are big enough to warrant special treatment or funding. Both cultures believe that when levels of achievement are low, higher academic standards should be applied to all students.

But the radical idea that all children can learn if they are taught well is not popular among North America's progressive educators. Siegfried Engelmann, the author of more than thirty instructional programs for hard-to-teach children, contends that educators support a "sorting-machine philosophy" like special education because it "considers the decision-makers first" rather than the children.

To support his argument, Engelmann cites a remarkable study by U.S. researcher Galen Alessi. In 1988 Alessi asked fifty school psychologists to identify the original reasons for their referral of a total of five thousand students into special education classes. Alessi found that faulty curricula, bad teaching practices, and inept school administration rarely accounted for the referrals. Instead home environment or some defect in the child accounted for almost all the slotting. "The results tend to leave little doubt about whether school psychologists work for the schools or the children," says Engelmann.

5. The most recent example of the progressive colonization of public schools is British Columbia's Year 2000 reform package. Reflecting American trends, this ambitious kindergarten to Grade 12 program seeks to replace grades, classrooms, and subjects with "learning environments" in which children of varying ages and skill levels all do their own thing at their own pace. The program, now supported by more than 450 documents, studiously avoids the words "challenge," "study," or "students." There are no standards. Typical of much progressive dogma, Year 2000 assumes that learning is simply a matter of playfully building on the intellectual and experiential capital that children bring to school. Such an élitist, upper middle-class notion is not only a contradiction of the very purpose of a public school, but a refutation of the meaning of the word education: "to lead out."

6. See Donald Hayes in *Nature*, April 30, 1992, pp. 739-740. Some of these statements are also based on personal communication with Donald Hayes.

7. Canada's dominant reading fad began as a philosophically complex movement among teachers in the early 1970s. Designed as an alternative to mindless worksheets and poorly designed look-and-say readers (such as the Dick and Jane readers), whole language sought to provide children with material that was worth reading and that respected their interests. It also sought to make reading and writing something that mattered in all subjects areas right across the curriculum.

These worthy goals, however, were undermined by thoughtless methodology. Whole language has always been more of a religious philosophy for teachers than a program of instruction for children. To this day, many of its theorists (such as Ken Goodman and Frank Smith) still maintain that all children can learn how to read "real books" by osmosis — or failing that, by predicting meaning from the story, using picture clues, or guessing. Education faculties still teach four dogmas that make "whole language" an ineffective and indirect approach for many children:

I. *Phonics should be taught incidentally or not at all.* For nearly three thousand years, conscientious reading teachers have begun reading instruction with the alphabet and sound-letter matches because it worked better that way. So, too, have Third World adult literacy crusaders as philosophically distinct as the Brazilian Marxist Paulo Friere or the Christian missionary Frank Laubach.

The importance of the phonetic tradition has been verified by hundreds of studies. The most recent was Marilyn Jager Adams's monumental 1990 report for the U.S. Senate (*Beginning to Read*). Adams, a cognitive psychologist at the Center for the Study of Reading at the University of Illinois and North America's premier reading expert, found that step-by-step phonetic instruction when included with the reading of meaningful stories "results in superior reading achievement overall, for both low-readiness and better prepared students."

2. *Learning how to read is as natural a process as learning how to speak.* Many whole language enthusiasts still insist that children should be left to their own devices: "They'll read when they are ready," goes the rhetoric. But printed text, which is not really a language at all, is a cultural invention that one must learn how to decode. As a January article in *Role Call*, a Toronto teachers' journal, recently noted, children who appear to read naturally at school have already had an average of two thousand hours of private instruction at home, where parents have encouraged them to pay attention to letters and words during the bedtime ritual of reading stories.

3. *Teaching spelling is unnecessary.* Some teachers now argue that computers will take care of a student's spelling needs. But such shortsightedness forgets that teachers throughout the ages have focused on spelling drills (and often unwieldy ones) because good readers use spelling patterns as a way to recognize and sound out new words. Simply put, spelling reinforces word recognition and builds reading vocabulary. To not draw attention to spelling, then, is to undermine a reading program.

4. *Children should choose their own reading material.* Many ministries of education and school boards have abandoned graded and sequential beginning reading series on this basis. This decision, however, penalizes children who need the kind of structured lessons and practice that a good reading series can provide. Several educational ministries have further aggravated this situation by limiting the selection of approved readers to "whole lan-

guage" only. The remaining provinces offer one or two phonetic reading series of not particularly high quality. (No Canadian phonetic reader now exists.)

The ongoing and endless debate about whole language versus phonics is misleading and useless. Good teachers have always known that a careful combination of whole language and direct instruction in phonics ensures that children can read so they can read to learn.

8. Open Court, now under revision by Marilyn Jager Adams, is published by the Open Court Publishing Company: P.O. Box 599 Peru, Illinois, 61354-0599; 1-815-223-2520.

9. Josef Macek actually published two interesting studies. The first, "Manitoba's Educational System and Its Current Impact," examined the science curriculum. The second and briefer study, "Towards a Better Education," suggests a cogent program for school reform.

10. "International Comparisons in Education — Curriculum, Values and Lessons" was initiated by Dr. Joe Freedman, a determined school reformer, and the Alberta Chamber of Resources (ACR). For a copy of the 1992 report write: ACR, Suite 1410, Oxford Tower 10235, 101 Street, Edmonton, Alberta, Canada, T5J 3G1.

11. Charles Ledger and Fraser Simpson, two Ontario math teachers, have designed a highly effective program for the intermediate grades that avoids all the pitfalls of spiralling. It outperforms all other math series in building both basic skills and the ability to solve mathematical problems. For more information write: Spirit of Math, Suite 180, 4981 Highway 7 East, Unit 12A, Markham, Ontario, L3R 1N1: 416-940-0456.

12. Stevenson, pp. 30-32.

13. Kilpatrick, p. 22.

14. Sharon Sheehan, a public health nurse, asks a good question about sex education in a 1992 issue of *Christianity Today*: "When kids are asking for help to build a life with someone they love, how can we simply hand them a condom?" She also notes that most sex-ed programs are driven by adult stereotypes. "Many students are offended by the adult assumption that most teens are sexually active (50 per cent in Canada). One girl was so uncomfortable that she felt obliged to tell her Living Skills teacher that she was not sleeping with her boyfriend. Students have also been persuaded to think this of each other. 'Now if you see a

couple together, everyone says, "Oh, they are".' Another commented, 'It's like the adult world invading our world.'"

15. The almost total aversion progressive educators have for drill, memory work, or practice has long irked Margaret MacMillan, head of history at Ryerson Polytechnical Institute: "It is time to examine that tired article of faith (used) in the school system that creativity is killed by learning rules and that repetition is boring. We don't think so when it comes to sport. That is one area where we encourage mastery of basic skills through endless drills. Has anyone suggested that a hockey player who has learned how to stickhandle or skate is somehow less of a creative player?... Perhaps it is time for us to start treating education with the same seriousness with which we treat sport."

CHAPTER 3

1. The divorce of schools from community life has even taken on architectural overtones. Beginning in the 1960s and early 1970s educators built schools without windows—all based on the unproven notion that students could somehow concentrate better in enclosed boxes.

2. Parental abandonment of schools has taken many forms and has been fuelled by a variety of destructive social forces. In pursuit of self-interest, many adults no longer value marriage or even parenthood. As the traditional two-parent family increasingly gives way to single-parent or guardian relationships, more and more children arrive at school emotionally dead or unsettled. Public schools have attempted to deal with this social disaster by accepting it as a form of progressive change that merely requires the classroom to become more therapeutic in tone. (Most social studies texts no longer even use the words "wife," "husband," or "marriage.") But this "psychologization" of education is neither desirable nor sustainable. Notes Barbara Dafoe Whitehead, an American writer: "The family is responsible for teaching lessons of dependence, self-restraint, responsibility, and right conduct, which are essential to a free, democratic society. If the family fails in these tasks, then the entire experiment in democratic self-rule is jeopardized."

   Schools disembodied from community and families ultimately become as vulnerable to abuse as children orphaned by their parents.

Consider, for example, the residential schools set up for Indian children after World War I. The wards, by government decree, were plucked from their homes and neighbourhoods and entrusted to strangers often thousands of miles away. Their keepers, usually priests and nuns, often physically and sexually abused their vulnerable charges in an environment lacking true community constraints and responsibilities.

In accepting children from homes with absent parents or communities with no sense of place, the modern school merely becomes a type of day-care centre that invents the same set of deplorable conditions. Well-intended teachers, armed with therapies and questionable classroom practices, end up operating with impunity and no community control. Sooner or later, the door to academic, emotional, or physical abuse opens and closes with no public witnesses.

3. The growth of bureaucracy has affected all educational institutions. Community colleges, for example, typically employ as many non-teaching staff as teachers.

4. John Chubb and Terry Moe's powerful but flawed argument for an overhaul of the public school system is called *Politics, Markets and America's Schools*. The authors correctly identify many of the problems but propose solutions (school vouchers) that are highly problematic.

5. These findings appear in Reginald Bibby's excellent book, *Teen Trends: A Nation in Motion*.

6. The famous Peter Principle, which states that individuals rise to their level of incompetence in a hierarchy, was originally based on studies of teacher competence.

7. Mortimer Smith, an American educator and one of the founders of the Council for Basic Education, called this jargon "educanto" or "mumbo jumbo developed by educators to confound the public in general and inquisitive parents in particular."

8. For more information on the dismal state of teacher training, read Rita Kramer's *Ed School Follies* or my own investigation, "Why Our Teachers Can't Teach" in *Quest Magazine* (September 1984).

9. The aversion to good experimental research with verifiable results is actually a contradiction of the progressive tradition. In championing activity, freedom, and discovery learning, most early progressives, including John Dewey, believed their schools should be subject to thorough field trials. The conclusions of such research, however, have never

been favourable. In a survey of five major English studies on progressive schools, researcher William Anthony found "a gradual apparent decline in the value of programs" over a period of sixty years largely due to stricter judgements of effectiveness. Anthony also concluded that "progressive methods are not generally superior to non-progressive methods for the teaching of reading and English, and that progressive methods are generally inferior to non-progressive methods for the teaching of arithmetic." (Bernbaum, pp. 149-181)

10. In some quarters, Discovery Math has been replaced by "lateral thinking." According to Dr. Peggy Means McIntosh of Wellesley College, too many math and science classes have been brutalized by "vertical thinking"—the idea that decisiveness or the mastery of something matters. If a child can't add 1+3+5, don't worry or teach him, says McIntosh, for in a lateral world, "the aim is not to win, but to be in a decent relationship with the invisible elements of the universe." School boards actually pay McIntosh $1,750 to help teachers help children "get off the right-wrong axis."

11. Reported in "Meta-Analysis in Education" by James Kulik and Chen-Lin Kulik in the *International Journal of Educational Research*, 1989, pp. 287-288.

12. The failure of computers to assist in learning or in even promoting "computer literacy" is well noted in educational journals. In *Technology Review* (January 1991), MIT researcher Ronni Rosenberg bluntly states that "computer literacy" as a fundamental skill "is oversold, misapplied and basically trivial in most schools." See also "Use of Technology in Schools: Still Elusive" (*Educational Digest*, May 1992), "Effectiveness of the Computer in the Teaching of Secondary School Mathematics" (*Educational Technology*, August 1992), "National Trends in Computer Use Among Canadian Secondary School Students: Implications for Cross-Cultural Analyses" (*Journal of Research on Computing in Education*, Fall 1989), and "Equity and Computers in the Schools: A Decade of Research" (*Research of Educational Research*, Winter 1991).

13. Englemann, p. 85.

14. The central tenet of this idiocy is that schools should be concerned only about process or "how to learn." British Columbia's controversial Year 2000 program exemplifies this progressive bias by never once mentioning results or the thing produced. Observed one critic: "I am

concerned about a system of schooling that places the acquisition of (learning) techniques above the acquisition of learning."

15. Case Vanderwolf, a professor at the University of Western Ontario, did the sleuthing and found "massive dissatisfaction" with the system.

16. John McMurtry, a professor at the University of Guelph, addressed this issue in the *Canadian Association of University Teachers' Bulletin* (February 1993): "The consumer-market model of education has become increasingly dominant, and now threatens to undermine the educational process.... If we are serious about the much more demanding business of teaching and learning, which requires that people do not consume but earn their knowledge, we will have to get underneath opinions to what students have in fact learned from the teaching of their instructors."

CHAPTER FOUR

1. An analysis of the 1990 National Assessment of Educational Progress math exams shows that private American schools suffer the same malaise as their public counterparts. The NAEP math's data for fourth, eighth, and twelfth graders showed students in private, Catholic, and public schools "achieving at disastrously low levels." Only a seven-point difference in average scores separated private from public schools—not much of a difference at all. Canadian parents who have examined provincial school profiles of both private and public schools have reported similar findings to me.

CHAPTER FIVE

1. A publication of the British Columbia Teachers Association for Excellence in Education makes this point, adding that the "teacher evaluation process has been handcuffed to the extent that administrators seldom write unsatisfactory reports on teachers. To avoid union challenges and grievances, many administrators elect instead to write vague reports on incompetent teachers or encourage transfers to other schools." In the public school system, these transfers are referred to as "the turkey trot."

2. From an essay by Doug Carnine titled "Teacher Directed Constructivism for Higher Order Thinking." For inquiries phone/fax: 503-683-7543.

3. Lisa Delpit, a Mississippi teacher, writes in the *Harvard Educational Review* (1988) about this problem boldly: "Several Black teachers have said to me recently that as much as they'd like to believe otherwise, they cannot help but conclude that many of the 'progressive' educational strategies imposed by liberals upon Black and poor children could only be based on a desire to ensure that the liberals' children get sole access to the dwindling pool of American jobs. Some have added that the liberal educators believe themselves to be operating with good intentions, but that these good intentions are only conscious delusions about their unconscious true motives."

4. For a unit on forests, British Columbia's Year 2000 program suggests this kind of integration:
Art: make paper
Social Studies: write letters to the editor about environmental issues
Language: listen to stories by and about Emily Carr
Music: dance to music from the Four Seasons by Vivaldi
Nutrition: write a guide for the library about edible plants in the forest
Science: make a class terrarium
Mathematics: use natural objects from the forest environment to develop concepts such as estimation and seriation

   A review of this odd collection of activities pointedly noted that "it is unclear that their connections are educationally meaningful ones.... In the forest example increased understanding promoted by any of the suggested activities contributes nothing to an understanding of any of the other supposedly related topics."

5. For more on the Whittle project, read "Dim Bulb" by Sara Mosle in *The New Republic*, January 18, 1993.

A Short Bibliography

CHAPTER ONE

Castle, E.B. *Ancient Education and Today.* Baltimore: Penguin Books, 1961.

Dobson, J.F. *Ancient Education and Its Meaning to Us.* Cooper Square Publishers Inc.: New York, 1963.

Filler, Louis. *Horace Mann on the Crisis in Education.* Yellow Springs: The Antioch Press, 1965.

Graves, Frank. *A History of Education Before the Middle Ages.* New York: The Macmillan Company, 1909.

Gwynne-Thomas, E.H. *A Concise History of Education to 1900 A.D.* Washington, D.C.: University Press of America, 1981.

Leon-Portilla, Miguel. *Aztec Thought and Culture.* Norman, Oklahoma: University of Oklahoma Press, 1963.

Mann, Horace. *The Republic and the School: On the Education of Free Men* (edited by Lawrence A. Cremin). New York: Teachers College Press, 1957.

Monroe, Paul. *A Brief Course in the History of Education.* New York: The Macmillan Company, 1909.

Neatby, Hilda. *So Little for the Mind.* Toronto: Clarke, Irwin and Company Limited, 1953.

Neatby, Hilda. *A Temperate Dispute.* Toronto: Clarke, Irwin and Company, 1954.

Postman, Neil. *Conscientious Objections: Stirring Up Trouble About Language, Technology and Education.* New York: Vintage Books, 1988.

Postman, Neil. *Technopoly: The Surrender of Culture to Technology.* New York: Alfred A. Knopf, 1992.

Sloane, Eric. *The Little Red School House.* Garden City, New York: Doubleday and Company, 1972.

Small, W.M. *Quintilian on Education.* Oxford: Clarendon Press, 1938.

CHAPTER TWO

Archambault, Reginald Donat. *Dewey on Education: Appraisals.* New York: Random House, 1966.

Barzun, Jacques. *Begin Here: The Forgotten Conditions of Teaching and Learning.* Chicago: University of Chicago Press, 1991.

Bereiter, Carl. *Must We Educate?* Englewood Cliffs, New Jersey: Prentice-Hall, Inc., 1973.

Botstein, Leon. "Damaged Literacy." *Daedalus* (119).2 (Spring 1990), pp. 55-84.

Cayley, David. *Northrop Frye in Conversation.* Toronto: Anansi, 1992.

Cassivi, Dennis. *Education and the Cult of Modernism: A Personal Observation.* Sydney, Nova Scotia: Angeline Enterprises, 1981.

Cremin, Lawrence. *Public Education.* New York: Basic Books, 1976.

Ellul, Jacques. *The Technological Society.* New York: Alfred A. Knopf, 1964.

Ellul, Jacques. *The Humiliation of the Word.* Grand Rapids, Michigan: William B. Eerdmans Publishing Company, 1985.

Huxley, Aldous. *Tomorrow and Tomorrow and Tomorrow and Other Essays.* New York: Harper & Row, 1972.

Kilpatrick, William. *Why Johnny Can't Tell Right From Wrong.* Toronto: Simon & Schuster, 1992.

Lawr, Douglas, and Gidney, Robert (eds.) *Educating Canadians: A Documentary History of Public Education.* Toronto: Van Nostrand Reinhold Ltd., 1973.

Lasch, Christopher. *The True and Only Heaven: Progress and Its Critics.* New York: W.W. Norton & Company, 1991.

Lasch, Christopher. *The Culture of Narcissism: American Life in an Age of Diminishing Expectations.* New York: Warner Books, 1979.

Mathews, Mitford. *Teaching to Read Historically Considered.* Chicago: University of Chicago Press, 1966.

Peters, Richard (ed.). *Perspectives on Plowden.* New York: Humanities Press, 1969.

Stevenson, Harold, and Stigler, James. *The Learning Gap: Why Our Schools Are Failing and What We Can Learn From Japanese and Chinese Education.* New York: Summit Books, 1992.

Toch, Thomas. *In the Name of Excellence: The Struggle to Reform the Nation's Schools, Why It's Failing and What Should Be Done.* New York: Oxford University Press, 1991.

Westerhoff, John H. III. *McGuffey and His Readers: Piety, Morality and Education in Nineteenth-Century America.* Nashville: Abingdon, 1978.

CHAPTER THREE

Bernbaum, Gerald (ed.). *Schooling in Decline.* London: The Macmillan Press Ltd., 1979.

Berry, Wendell. *Home Economics.* San Francisco: North Point Press, 1987.

Berry, Wendell. *What Are People For.* San Francisco: North Point Press, 1990.

Chubb, John, and Moe, Terry. *Politics, Markets and America's Schools.* Washington, D.C.: The Brookings Institution, 1990.

Coleman, Peter, and Larocque, Linda. *Struggling to Be "Good Enough."* London: The Falmer Press, 1990.

Dixon, Des. *Future Schools and How to Get There from Here: A Primer for Evolutionaries.* Toronto: ECW Press, 1992.

Engelmann, Siegfried. *War Against the Schools' Academic Child Abuse.* Portland, Oregon: Halcyon House, 1992.

Finn, Chester. *We Must Take Charge: Our Schools and Our Future.* Toronto: Maxwell Macmillan, 1991.

Feinberg, Walter. *Reason and Rhetoric: The Intellectual Foundations of 20th Century Liberal Educational Policy.* Toronto: John Wiley and Sons, Inc., 1975.

Hill, Paul, et al. *High Schools with Character.* (R-3944-RC). Santa Monica: The Rand Corporation, 1990.

Hillocks, George. "What Works in Teaching Composition: A Meta-analysis of Experimental Treatment Studies." *American Journal of Education,* November 1984, pp. 133-165.

Illich, Ivan. *Deschooling Society.* New York: Harper & Row, 1970.

Illich, Ivan, and Verne, Etienne. *Imprisoned in the Global Classroom.* London: Writers and Readers Publishing Cooperative, 1976.

Kramer, Rita. *Ed School Follies: The Miseducation of America's Teacher.* Toronto: Maxwell Macmillan, 1991.

Powell, Arthur. *The Shopping Mall High School: Winners and Losers in the Educational Marketplace.* Boston: Houghton Mifflin Company, 1985.

Rosak, Theodore. *The Cult of Information.* New York: Pantheon Books, 1986.

CHAPTER FOUR

Benjamin, Robert. *Making Schools Work: A Reporter's Journey Through Some of America's Most Remarkable Classrooms.* New York: Continuum Publishing Corporation, 1981.

Coleman, James, and Hoffer, Thomas. *Public and Private High Schools: The Impact of Communities.* New York: Basic Books Inc., 1987.

Enochs, James. "The Restoration of Standards: The Modesto Plan." *Fastback 129,* Bloomington, Indiana: Phi Delta Kappa Educational Foundation, 1979.

Frye, Northrop. *On Education.* Toronto: Fitzhenry & Whiteside, 1988.

Grant, Gerald. "The Character of Education and the Education of Character." *Daedalus* (1981), pp. 135-149.

Hardin, Garrett. *Filters Against Folly.* New York: Penguin Books, 1986.

Holmes, Mark, et al. (eds.) *Educational Policy for Effective Schools.* Toronto: OISE Press, 1989.

Holmes, Mark, and Wynne, Edward. *Making the School an Effective Community.* New York: Falmer Press, 1989.

Rutter, Michael, et al. *Fifteen Thousand Hours: Secondary Schools and Their Effects on Children.* Cambridge: Harvard University Press, 1979.

CHAPTER FIVE

Adams, Marilyn Jager. *Beginning to Read: Thinking and Learning about Print: A Summary.* Urbana, Illinois: Center for the Study of Reading; University of Illinois at Urbana-Champaign: The Reading Research and Education Center, 1990.

Becker, Wesley (ed.). "Direct Instruction: A General Case for Teaching the General Case." *Education and Treatment of Children* (11) 4 (November 1988), pp. 301-401.

Cuban, Larry. "The Corporate Myth of Reforming Public Schools." Phi Delta Kappan, (October, 1992) pp. 157-159.

Etzioni, Amitai. *The Spirit of Community: Rights, Responsibilities and the Communitarian Agenda.* New York: Crown Publishers, 1993.

Lasch, Christopher. "Why Liberalism Lacks Virtue." *New Perspectives Quarterly* (8) 2, (Spring 1991), pp. 30-34.

O'Neill, G. Patrick. "Teaching Effectiveness: A Review of the Research." *Canadian Journal of Education* (13) 1, pp. 162-178, 1988.

Whitehead, Barabara Dafoe. "Dan Quayle Was Right." *The Atlantic Monthly* (271) 4 (April 1993), pp. 47-84.

Whitehead, Barbara Dafoe. "The New Family Values." *Utne Reader* 57 (May/June 1993), pp. 61-65.

Index

This book is set in Centaur typeface. Designed by Bruce Rogers, it was first introduced in 1929. Centaur is a versatile typeface that makes a distinctive and elegant impression. The italic type is Arrighi and is based on a design made by Frederic Warde.

Electronic paging by Valerie Van Volkenburg and David Murphy
Cover and text design by Brant Cowie / ArtPlus Limited